THE ULTIMATE GUIDE TO STATE & COUNTY RV CAMPING

DISCOVER AFFORDABLE, HIDDEN GEMS IN COUNTY, MUNICIPAL & CITY PARKS —THE HASSLE-FREE RV ROAD TRIP GUIDE FOR TIME-SAVING ADVENTURES!

WANDA WHEELER

TABLE OF CONTENTS

INTRODUCTION

Five years ago, I was comfortably settled in a picturesque area of a state park in the Blue Ridge Mountains. One early morning, as I opened my RV door, I was delighted to see a family of deer grazing just a few feet away. The mist was lifting, the birds were starting their morning chorus, and I felt incredibly lucky to call this my backyard. That moment, along with many others, reaffirmed my choice of the RV lifestyle and underscored why state and county parks are my preferred camping locations. They provide an experi- ence that private campgrounds often cannot offer—pure, unblem- ished nature.'

I've spent five fantastic years as a full-time RVer, and what a remark- able journey it has been! I've parked in lively cities and serene forests, but the true enchantment lies in state and county parks. These loca- tions boast a natural beauty that's truly unmatched. The trees,   wildlife, and vast open areas foster a real connection to the great outdoors. This book is designed to be your comprehensive guide to affordable RV camping in these parks. I'm here to assist you in saving time and money while exploring hidden gems across the nation. Whether you're a veteran traveler or just getting started, you'll find the tips and insights you need for enjoyable adventures.

Who would benefit from this book? It's designed for anyone passionate about the outdoors! If you're an RV traveler seeking fresh adventures, a retiree wanting to explore the nation, or a family plan- ning a memorable road trip, you'll uncover a wealth of information. Budget- minded travelers will find great value in the affordable options, while those craving adventure will enjoy discovering hidden gems. Digital nomads will also find locations with good internet access for a seamless work-cation experience.

State and county parks bring many benefits you might not find at private campgrounds. For one, the scenic landscapes are truly remarkable. Imagine starting your day with a lakeside sunrise or setting up your tent surrounded by tall pines. These parks often provide generous camping spaces, which are great for larger rigs. Many also welcome pets, so you can take your four-legged friends along. Being near local attractions means you can venture out to explore quaint towns, hiking trails, and historical sites. Moreover, the natural settings offer fantastic chances for wildlife viewing and tranquil getaways, providing a peaceful and relaxing environment for your adventures.

The book is structured with user-friendly chapters, each dedicated to various elements of RV camping in state and county parks. You'll discover sections on trip planning, finding your way to your destination, and getting to know the available amenities. Additionally, we'll explore enjoyable activities, eco-conscious practices to adopt, and essential safety advice. You'll also find a wealth of insider tips from my personal experiences to enhance your journey.

The RV lifestyle thrives on community. Connecting with fellow campers, swapping stories, and learning from each other adds a unique flavor to this journey. You should reach out to other RV lovers in person at a park or via online communities. This book is intended to cultivate that feeling of belonging and friendship among all RV enthusiasts.

Rest assured, the information in this book is thoroughly researched and verified. You'll find up-to-date contact details, accurate maps, and firsthand experiences to guide you. I've spent countless hours compiling this information to ensure it's reliable and useful so you can embark on your adventures with confidence and peace of mind.

Think of this book as your trusty, user-friendly guide. Each chapter is packed with actionable tips, detailed park listings, and useful resources. Whether you're flipping through it on the road or reading it at home, you'll find it easy to navigate and full of handy informa- tion, making your RV journey a breeze.

As you journey through these pages, I hope you're inspired to start your own RV adventures. My time spent exploring state and county parks has been incredibly rewarding, and I believe it can bring you joy as well. So load up your RV, hit the open road, and get prepared to uncover some of the most stunning and peaceful places our nation has in store. Enjoy your camping adventures!

CHAPTER 1

PLANNING YOUR RV CAMPING ADVENTURE

A couple of years ago, I found this awesome little state park in Arkansas called Petit Jean State Park, where I parked my RV. It was tucked away among trees and had some stunning mountain views. It was the perfect escape. I can still picture those early morn- ings when I'd grab my coffee and step outside, feeling that refreshing mountain air. The birds were singing, and a light breeze was dancing through the leaves, making everything feel so peaceful, like time stood still. That trip really hit home for me: RV camping is all about soaking in the whole experience, not just reaching a destination.

In the last five years, I've been on quite a few adventures and picked up some valuable tips for planning RV trips. I've checked out tons of state and county parks, each one offering its own special vibe. This section is here to guide you in planning your RV camping journey, whether you're after a quick weekend escape or a month-long road trip. Let's jump into how to set your camping goals, figure out how long you want to be away and find activities that match your interests.

1.1 SETTING YOUR CAMPING GOALS

When gearing up for your RV camping journey, the first thing to consider is what you hope to achieve. This insight will help you shape your plans to fulfill your aspirations, promising a fantastic experience. Are you planning on relaxing and unwinding or seeking excitement and adventure? You may want to explore the great outdoors and spot some wildlife, or your main goal may be to bond with family and create unforgettable moments together.

If personal relaxation is your goal, consider parks known for their peaceful settings. Consider choosing a peaceful lakeside location or a hidden nook in the forest. Pack a captivating book and a hammock, and immerse yourself in the calming ambiance of nature. Alterna- tively, if you crave excitement, seek out parks that feature tough hiking paths, rock climbing, or water activities. For instance, Cathe- dral Gorge State Park in Nevada, known for its unique clay forma- tions and caves, provides an abundance of adventure.

Venturing into the beauty of nature and wildlife is a wonderful aspi- ration! Many state and county parks are home to rich ecosystems and plentiful wildlife. Spend your days bird watching, hiking through lush forests, or taking pictures of stunning landscapes. For example,

Gooseberry Falls State Park in Minnesota, famous for its waterfalls and trails, is perfect for nature lovers. Lastly, if family bonding is your aim, choose parks with activities for all ages. Look for areas with playgrounds, simple hiking trails, and educational programs. Engaging in activities like fishing, kayaking, and guided nature walks can lead to wonderful family experiences.

After determining your goals, the next thing to consider is the dura- tion of your trip. A weekend escape is ideal for a brief refresh and a chance to unwind, plus it demands minimal planning and packing— great for those with hectic lives A week-long journey provides a nice mix of excitement and downtime, allowing you to experience different activities without the rush. If you're considering an extended trip or full-time RV living, you'll need to plan more thoroughly. Longer trips provide the opportunity to explore several parks and locations, helping you form a stronger bond with each destination.

Identifying desired activities is crucial for a fulfilling trip. If you love hiking and nature trails, look for parks with well-maintained paths and scenic views. Fishing and water sports enthusiasts should seek out parks with lakes, rivers, or ocean access. Salmon Lake State Park in Montana is a great example, providing fantastic fishing opportuni- ties amidst stunning scenery. Additionally, bird watching and wildlife observation can be very rewarding experiences. Check out parks known for their biodiversity and habitats that attract various species. Local cultural and historical sites add another layer of interest to your trip. Explore nearby towns, museums, and landmarks to enrich your experience.

Setting realistic expectations is key to enjoying your RV camping adventure. It's easy to get carried away with ambitious plans, but remember to pace yourself. If you're a beginner, try starting with shorter excursions to gradually get used to RV life. Seasoned RVers might plan more elaborate adventures, but leaving room for spon- taneity is important. Nature can be unpredictable, and sometimes, the best moments are unplanned. Stay flexible and manage your expectations. If you run into bad weather or an unexpected roadblock, view it as an opportunity to explore something different.

Preparing for your RV camping trip ultimately involves matching your objectives with your plans and staying flexible for unexpected opportunities. Setting specific objectives and planning effectively will maximize your travel experience, whether you aim to unwind, seek thrills, or bond with loved ones. Excited about the planning ahead!

1.2 CHOOSING THE RIGHT STATE AND COUNTY PARKS FOR YOUR NEEDS

Choosing the correct state or county park for your RV camping experience can significantly impact the success of your trip. One initial factor to consider is the presence of amenities suitable for RVs. Search for parks that provide water, electricity, and sewer connections. These make your stay much more comfortable and convenient. For instance, DeSoto State Park in Alabama offers these amenities and a beautiful setting with fall foliage and waterfalls. Additionally, having access to dump stations is crucial for managing waste during extended stays.

A pet-friendly environment is crucial, especially when bringing your beloved furry friends while traveling. Certain parks enforce specific regulations, like leash mandates or designated pet zones. Knowing these regulations in advance can prevent you from facing unforeseen difficulties. For instance, Petit Jean State Park in Arkansas welcomes pets and offers numerous trails for you and your furry companion to enjoy a relaxing stroll. Visit the park's website or call them before- hand to know their rules for bringing your pet.

If you have a large rig, ease of access and suitability are vital. Parks with narrow roads or tight turns can be challenging to navigate. Search for parks with pull-through spots and plenty of room for maneuvering. For instance, Wallowa Lake State Park in Oregon offers full hookup sites and heated bathrooms, making it an excellent option for bigger RVs. Additionally, being close to nearby attractions and activities can improve your overall experience. Having choices for day trips, such as a hiking trail, a historical site, or a charming town nearby, can enhance your adventure experience.

Researching parks may appear overwhelming, yet it doesn't have to be. Begin by making use of official park websites and databases. These frequently offer the most precise and current information. Portals like the Palo Duro Canyon State Park website in Texas provide informa- tion about facilities, costs, and options for things to do. Next, dive into user reviews and ratings on camping forums. Fellow campers often share valuable insights and tips that you won't find on official websites. Lastly, don't hesitate to contact park offices directly. Park rangers and staff can provide firsthand information about current conditions, upcoming events, and any recent changes.

Comprehending and following park regulations and rules are essen- tial for a hassle-free visit. Every park establishes its own regulations on maximum length of stay, booking guidelines, and other restric- tions. For example, some parks might limit stays to 14 days out of every 30 days to ensure all visitors have equal opportunity to enjoy   the park. Rules concerning campfires, noise levels, and waste disposal are implemented to protect the environment and guarantee an enjoy- able experience for all guests. Make sure to acquaint yourself with these rules before you reach your destination. This consists of safety regulations and wildlife procedures. Certain parks, such as those located in areas with bears, enforce particular regulations on food storage to avoid interactions with wildlife.

I've had the pleasure of exploring many parks, and I've gathered some personal insights and recommendations. Take Smallwood State Park in Maryland, for instance. Located just an hour south of Washington, D.C., it's a fantastic spot with wooded sites, electric hookups, and walking trails. For those interested in geological wonders, Cathedral Gorge State Park in Nevada offers unique bentonite clay formations and caves. If fishing is your thing, Salmon Lake State Park in Montana is a must-visit, nestled between Glacier and Yellowstone with excel- lent lake and river fishing.

For those looking for hidden gems, consider Kodachrome Basin State Park in Utah. It is very close to Bryce Canyon National Park but much less crowded, providing a peaceful retreat with stunning scenery. Another highlight is Falling Waters State Park in Florida, featuring the state's tallest waterfall and offers a relaxed camping experience with 24 spacious campsites. Selecting the correct park may require investigation and organization, but the payoff is worth it. You can find parks that meet and exceed your expectations by considering your needs and preferences and leveraging available resources. Happy camping!

1.3 UNDERSTANDING PARK FEES AND RESERVATION SYSTEM

Understanding the puzzle of navigating fee structures and reservation systems for state and county parks can make everything fall into place. When talking about costs, you will come across various kinds. Many parks frequently require entrance fees and daily usage fees. These fees cover only the entrance to the park, typically varying from a couple of dollars to $20, based on the specific park and location. In Arizona, state parks usually have an entrance fee that can range from no charge to approximately $20 to help with the upkeep of park services and features.

Camping fees are definitely something to keep in mind. They vary based on the campground's features. If you're going for a no-frills experience, primitive sites can cost around $10 to $15 a night. But if you want water and electric hookups, expect to pay between $30 and
$60 per night. And don't forget about those extra charges for laundry, showers, or Wi-Fi—they can really bump up your total. Take DeSoto State Park in Alabama, for instance; it offers many amenities that justify the higher camping fees, making your stay more enjoyable.

Discount programs are available at numerous parks for seniors, veterans, and regular campers. These programs allow for substantial cost reductions and increase the affordability of RV camping. States such as Georgia provide different discounts, such as Snowbirds Special and military discounts. It is advisable to visit the park's official website or contact them directly to find out about potential discounts for which you qualify. Membership options such as the National Park Pass can provide significant benefits, particularly if you frequent several parks yearly. These tickets frequently offer savings on admission costs and additional services.

Efficiently booking reservations is essential for a seamless and relaxed camping trip. The majority of state and county parks now utilize online reservation systems and booking platforms. Platforms such as ReserveAmerica and Recreation.gov enable users to browse for open campsites, view images of the locations, and make early reservations. Making reservations ahead of time is especially crucial during busy times such as summer and holiday weekends when parks can reach full capacity rapidly. It is smart to plan ahead since certain parks allow reservations up to a year in advance.

Should you require a reservation at the last minute, choices are still available. Several parks offer limited spaces for spontaneous visitors or same-day reservations. If there have been cancellations, contacting the park office directly may result in securing a reservation. Being open to changing dates and visiting less crowded parks can also improve your chances of securing a reservation.

It is important to comprehend cancellation and refund policies to prevent surprise fees. Every park has specific rules regarding the refund and rescheduling processes. Usually, you must cancel within a specific time window, 48 to 72 hours before your check-in date, to get a full or partial refund. Rules regarding missed appointments and leaving early differ; however, one night's fee is typically non-refund- able. Certain parks provide insurance choices for canceling trips, which can save you in case unforeseen circumstances make you alter your plans.

Successfully controlling expenses and maximizing the benefits of park accommodations requires some strategic planning. Search for parks that provide combined service deals, including firewood, guided tours, or equipment rentals at a reduced price. Traveling during periods of low demand can lead to reduced prices and less crowded destinations. For example, going to parks during the off- peak seasons of spring and fall can offer a quieter visit and help you cut costs.

Taking advantage of membership programs such as the National Park Pass or state-specific annual passes can result in substantial savings, especially for those who camp often. These programs frequently include admission fees and offer reduced rates on camping and other facilities. It is also valuable to consider the loyalty programs provided by certain parks, as they offer discounted rates or complimentary nights to returning guests.

Understanding park fees and reservation systems allows you to make informed decisions and plan a more enjoyable and budget-friendly RV camping adventure.

1.4 SEASONAL TIPS: BEST TIMES TO VISIT STATE PARKS

Knowing how various seasons impact your RV camping adventure is essential for coordinating a journey that meets your requirements. Weather and climate are important factors in deciding when to visit state parks. In the winter season, parks in the north can be covered in snow, ideal for winter sports enthusiasts who like snowshoeing or cross-country skiing. Nevertheless, the low temperatures can bring difficulties like frozen pipes or restricted access to specific areas in the park. However, summer also provides extended daylight hours and pleasant temperatures, perfect for engaging in water activities like swimming, though it may also entail managing hot weather and busy parks.

Another aspect to take into account is the closure of parks for seasonal maintenance. During the off-season, some parks shut down specific facilities or whole sections for maintenance or weather- related reasons. For example, many parks in Alaska are only acces- sible in the summer because of the significant snowfall in winter. Looking up the park's website or contacting the park office before your visit can prevent you from finding your desired spot closed upon arrival. Peak and off-peak seasons can considerably impact your overall experience, too. Visiting in peak season, such as summer or holidays, typically results in more crowded campsites and increased costs. On the other hand, quiet and peaceful experiences can be enjoyed during less crowded times, such as the beginning of spring or the end of fall, along with the benefit of reduced expenses.

Seasonal attractions have the potential to create lasting memories during your adventures. During the spring season, wildflowers bloom abundantly, resulting in a stunning view. In locations such as Palo Duro Canyon State Park in Texas, vibrant flowers cover the area, transforming it into a vibrant masterpiece. Summer revolves around water sports - the season's main attractions are kayaking, paddle-boarding, and swimming. Parks that offer access to lakes, rivers, or the ocean are extremely popular for these enjoyable activities. When fall comes, the leaves changing colors bring a unique charm. Picturesque routes through destinations such as Letchworth State Park in New York, often referred to as the "Grand Canyon of the East," provide spectacular sights of autumn foliage. Typically, winter is a bit more peaceful, offering excellent chances to observe animals and appreciate the tranquility of snowy scenes. Mueller State Park in Colorado transforms into a winter wonderland, ideal for individuals seeking tranquility.

Preparing for your RV journey involves making seasonal changes to guarantee comfort and readiness. Prepare warm clothes and heating choices for the winter season. Consider using thermal layers, durable jackets, and portable heaters to maintain warmth in your RV. Summer requires light equipment and ways to stay cool. Staying cool can be achieved using breathable fabrics, carrying portable fans, and applying ample sunscreen. Spring weather is unpredictable, making rain gear and waterproof items essential. A high-quality raincoat, waterproof boots, and some tarps can be a lifesaver. Autumn's fluctu- ating temperatures require you to wear layered clothing. Bring a combination of short and long-sleeved shirts, sweaters, and a light jacket to be prepared for variable weather conditions.

Every season has specific safety factors to take into account. The high temperatures in summer may result in heat exhaustion. Therefore, it's crucial to keep yourself hydrated, choose suitable clothes, and rest in shaded areas. Sun protection is essential; a quality hat, sunglasses, and high-SPF sunscreen are necessary. Winter exposes individuals to the dangers of hypothermia and frostbite. Make sure your RV has enough heating, and bring along emergency blankets and hand warmers. Being ready for storms is crucial during the spring, especially if you live in an area that often experiences severe weather. Monitor weather predictions and prepare a strategy for finding refuge. Wildlife behavior may also change depending on the time of year. For instance, bears become increasingly active during autumn as they get ready for hibernation. Always securely store food and stay vigilant of your surroundings to prevent unexpected encounters.

Knowing about these seasonal changes and being ready can signifi- cantly improve your RV camping adventure. Each season provides distinct chances and obstacles, whether you are seeking out spring blossoms, plunging into summer waters, enjoying autumn hues, or embracing winter's tranquility. Considering weather conditions, park closures, and seasonal attractions can assist in planning a trip that meets your expectations and creates lasting memories.

1.5 CRAFTING CUSTOMIZABLE ITINERARIES

Developing a flexible and customizable itinerary can greatly enhance your RV trip planning experience. Beginning with short trips on weekends. These brief getaways are ideal for a quick yet satisfying break. Select parks a short drive from where you are to make the most of your time. Picture yourself going to Morro Bay State Park in California for a two-night stay. You can spend your initial day touring the nearby Hearst Castle and appreciating the coastal scenery. During day two, consider hiking around Morro Rock and renting a kayak. Maintaining a flexible schedule allows for unexpected deviations, such as dropping by a nearby farmer's market that caught your eye along the route.

Balancing is crucial for week-long adventures. You have sufficient time to investigate without experiencing any hurry. If you choose DeSoto State Park in Alabama, for example. Begin your week by spending a few days exploring the picturesque hiking trails and checking out the waterfalls. During the middle of the week, plan a day excursion to the nearby Little River Canyon for some adventurous white-water rafting. While returning, make a detour to the picturesque town of Mentone to enjoy some regional dishes and browse through the shops. The end of the week can be set aside for unwinding at your campsite, possibly even taking advantage of the park's seasonal pool. This mix of action and calmness creates a balanced vacation.

Long vacations provide the opportunity for a thorough exploration of several different places. Imagine a 30-day trip across the Pacific Northwest. Start your journey at Wallowa Lake State Park in Oregon, where you can enjoy a week of fishing and hiking in the Wallowa Mountains. Afterward, head to Mueller State Park in Colorado for stunning photo opportunities. Stay for an additional week to discover the paths and photograph the beautiful scenery. Proceed to Cathedral Gorge State Park in Nevada to admire its distinctive clay formations.

These long journeys give you the chance to fully experience each place, truly embracing the local culture and the natural scenery.

Building flexibility into your itinerary is crucial. Life on the road can be unpredictable, and a rigid schedule can lead to stress. Include buffer days for rest or unexpected delays. If you plan to visit three parks over ten days, consider making the eleventh day a rest day at a nearby town or even a spontaneous extra night at a park you particu- larly enjoyed. Alternative routes and backup plans are also vital. If you find that a particular park is overcrowded, have a list of nearby alter- natives. For instance, if Letchworth State Park in New York is full, you might head to the less crowded Stony Brook State Park nearby. Spontaneity can add an element of adventure, so watch for local events or attractions you might want to explore.

Certain places absolutely deserve a spot on your list of must-visit destinations. Renowned state parks such as Palo Duro Canyon State Park in Texas, which is recognized as the second largest canyon in the U.S., provide rugged rock formations and extensive trail networks. Lesser-known treasures, such as Falling Waters State Park in Florida, showcase the tallest waterfall in the state and offer a quieter environ- ment. Make sure not to dismiss local cultural and historical locations. When you're at Morro Bay State Park, exploring the nearby town of Cayucos, with its historic pier and charming shops, can enhance your experience.

Travel tips can make all the difference in optimizing your camping experience. Efficient route planning and navigation are essential. Use apps like Google Maps or RV-friendly navigation tools to plot your course, avoiding narrow roads or low bridges that might challenge your rig. Balancing driving time and relaxation is key. Aim for no more than four to five hours of driving per day to avoid fatigue and allow for sightseeing stops. Finding convenient rest stops and refu- eling points is also crucial. Apps like GasBuddy can help you locate the nearest fuel stations, while websites like FreeRoam can help you find rest areas and overnight parking spots.

Incorporating these tips into your RV camping plans will help you create an itinerary that is fulfilling and adaptable to whatever the road throws your way.

1.6 PACKING ESSENTIALS AND MUST-HAVE GEAR

Embarking on a journey in a recreational vehicle might appear daunting initially, but with proper preparation and a bit of order, it can be incredibly straightforward. Let's begin by focusing on your   true essentials. Important camping equipment should include tents, sleeping bags, and cozy chairs for relaxing nights next to the fire. Although you may intend to rest in your RV, having a tent can provide additional room for children or visitors or simply a peaceful spot to unwind and enjoy reading. Ensure your sleeping bags are appropriate for the season, whether the cool spring or the hot summer nights. Do not overlook a comfortable camping chair; it's essential for stargaz- ing, chatting, and savoring your morning coffee.

Having cooking appliances is essential. A portable stove is necessary for preparing meals while away from traditional amenities. Select a product that is simple to install and operate, and remember to bring along additional fuel. A durable set of utensils, pots, and pans will also be necessary. Coolers and airtight containers can assist in preserving food freshness and protecting it from wildlife. If you like cooking, consider bringing a portable grill for those ideal BBQ evenings outdoors. A collapsible sink can also simplify the process of washing dishes, allowing your RV's plumbing to remain available for other activities.

The following items to be listed are personal belongings. Bring appro- priate clothing that can be used for the weather and activities you have scheduled. Incorporate multiple clothing layers for varying temperatures and wear durable shoes for hiking or adventuring. Toiletries are necessary but think about using travel-sized options to conserve space. Remember to bring medications, including prescribed and non-prescribed, for common issues such as headaches or allergies. It is essential to have a properly equipped first aid kit with bandages, antiseptics, and other necessary medical supplies. Safety and emergency kits should also contain items such as a multi-tool, flashlights with spare batteries, and a fire extinguisher. These items can greatly impact your situation when you are distant from imme- diate assistance.

Customizing your packing list to cater to individual requirements can enhance the pleasure of your journey. Bring toys, games, and extra clothes for family vacations to keep the children happy and cozy. Having books or a portable DVD player can be incredibly helpful during idle periods. Gear specific to pet-friendly camping is neces- sary. Bring sufficient pet food, water bowls, leashes, and bedding to ensure your furry companions are comfortable. When preparing for adventure activities, make sure to bring along the essential equip- ment. Hikers should carry durable boots, hiking poles, and water- filled packs. Fishermen should bring their fishing gear, while photog- raphers need to carry their cameras, lenses, and tripods.

Optimizing space and staying organized are key to a smooth RV trip. Space-saving packing techniques, like rolling clothes instead of folding them, can free up vital room. Use storage solutions like stack- able containers, under-bed storage bins, and door organizers to keep everything in its place. Collapsible items, like bowls and containers, can also save space. Keeping frequently used items accessible is another smart move. Store these in easily reachable places to avoid digging through your stuff whenever you need something. Consider using drawer dividers and labeled bins to keep things tidy and easy to find.

Preparing for unexpected situations is a vital part of RV travel. Ensure you always carry additional parts and tools for repairs, like a tire repair kit, spare hoses, and a basic tool kit. This may help avoid numerous challenges in the event of any mishaps while driving. Equal importance should be placed on having additional supplies of food and water. Take additional non-perishable food and bottled water in excess of what is necessary for your journey. It is important to wear appropriate clothing for the current weather conditions. Pack sun hats, sunglasses, and plenty of sunscreen when you go on a summer vacation. On winter trips, thermal blankets and hand warmers can save the day.

In the end, a well-arranged RV is necessary for a seamless trip. By preparing ahead of time and customizing your packing to suit your needs, you will be prepared for various circumstances. This lets you focus on the key elements: enjoying the experience, connecting with nature, and creating lasting memories. Proper gear and a tidy RV can improve your travel, whether a brief weekend getaway or a month- long journey. Have fun packing, and may you have an even more joyful trip!

CHAPTER 2
NAVIGATING AND FINDING THE PERFECT CAMPSITES

One summer, I got disoriented in a maze of paths at an Oregon state park. As the sun was going down, creating long shadows, I experienced that familiar feeling of uncertainty. I had planned to go on a brief hike but ended up straying from the main trail. That is when I understood how crucial it is to grasp park layouts and utilize all resources to move around effectively. The experience gave me important lessons I am excited to pass on to you.

2.1 UNDERSTANDING STATE PARK LAYOUTS

Upon your initial arrival at a state park, you will typically come across the primary entrance and park office. You should visit these locations for information, maps, and any required supplies. The park office frequently serves as a visitor center, providing brochures, trail maps, and displays on the park's history and natural characteristics. Here is where you are able to inquire, receive the most recent information on trail conditions, and learn about any special events occurring while you are here.

Upon entry, you will observe that campgrounds are commonly separated into distinct areas. Certain parks feature individual sections designated for RVs, tents, and group camping. RV-specific areas typically provide electrical hookups, water, and occasionally sewer connections. These spaces are specifically created for bigger vehicles, featuring drive-through sites and plenty of room for slide-outs. On the flip side, tent camping areas are typically more isolated and immersed in the natural environment, offering a more rugged experience. Camping sites designed for groups are ideal for family reunions or get-togethers with friends, offering spacious sites and shared areas.

Recreational zones and facilities are spread out across the park. Picnic spots, playgrounds, and day-use areas are available for you to unwind and have a meal. Many parks also offer water access points and boat launch areas, perfect for fishing, kayaking, or just appreciating the scenery. Certain parks provide extra features such as pools, information centers, and nature activities, improving the quality of your visit.

Trails and natural landmarks are typically clearly labeled and easy to locate, yet it is crucial to become acquainted with the layout before setting off. Many parks provide a selection of paths, including simple routes suitable for families and more challenging trails that lead you far into nature. Typically, these trails offer access to natural attrac- tions such as lakes, rivers, waterfalls, and scenic viewpoints, allowing for adventure and exploration.

Identifying key zones within the park can make navigation much easier. Day-use areas and picnic spots are great for a quick lunch or a pit stop during hiking. These areas often have tables, grills, and some- times even shelters, making them perfect for a family outing. RV- specific zones and facilities are your home base, offering the comforts and conveniences you need for a longer stay. Knowing where these zones are can help you settle in quickly and start enjoying your trip.

Tent camping areas are typically situated in more remote locations, offering a peaceful, more immersive environment. These areas are usually located near hiking paths and organic elements, allowing you to awaken to the sounds of the natural world. Access points for water and places to launch boats are necessary if you intend to spend time on the water. Knowing the location of these points can enhance your adventure, whether you are kayaking, fishing, or swimming.

Park signs and markers are essential for finding your way around a state park. Trail markers show the route and level of challenge, aiding in selecting the appropriate trail suited to your skills and preferences. Signs pointing to bathrooms, picnic spots, and trail starting points are typically conveniently located and simple to understand. Trailhead information boards and maps offer important trail details such as length, elevation variations, and points of interest. Regularly checking these forums can assist you in staying focused and making well-informed choices about your path.

Getting around expansive parks can feel daunting, but there are tactics to simplify the process. It is a no-brainer to use park maps and visitor guides. These tools offer a graphical representation of the park, assisting in route planning and recognizing important sections. Planning your routes ahead of time can help you save time and avoid frustration upon arrival. Identifying landmarks and recording distances can assist in organizing your agenda and maximizing your visit.

Another helpful suggestion is to mentally note landmarks and reference points. Distinctive landmarks such as big boulders, rare trees, or where different paths meet can act as guides, assisting in retracing your steps after straying from the main route. It is a wise decision to ask for help from park rangers. Rangers possess expertise regarding the park and can offer valuable insights and recommendations. If you need help with directions or advice on the best trails and activities, feel free to ask for help.

Knowing the layout of state parks and utilizing available resources well can improve your camping experience, making it more enjoyable and less stressful. Take your time exploring, appreciate the beauty of nature, and savor every moment during your adventure.

2.2 UTILIZING DETAILED MAPS AND GPS COORDINATES

Having accurate maps and GPS coordinates is essential for a stress- free camping trip. It can be simple to become disoriented in the large area of a state park, particularly for newcomers. Precise navigation instruments keep you from getting off track and aid in locating particular campsites and facilities efficiently. Picture pulling into a park following a lengthy drive, only to search for your designated   spot for an additional hour. Effective paths for travel in the park can save time and minimize irritation, enabling you to appreciate your environment immediately.

Deciphering park maps may appear overwhelming initially; however, it becomes instinctive once you grasp the fundamentals. Begin with the key and icons on the map. These symbols depict different ameni- ties and environmental characteristics, such as bathrooms, areas for picnicking, and paths. Using a map scale is extremely helpful for measuring distances accurately. It assists in converting the map's measurements to actual distances, aiding in the precise planning of hikes or drives. Contour lines display shifts in height, illustrating which paths are level and steep. This is particularly handy for those preparing for a hike and wishing to steer clear of excessively chal- lenging trails. Many maps include a north arrow or compass to assist in orienting yourself and navigating trail intersections.

GPS technology has completely transformed the way we navigate through state parks. By having devices and apps easily accessible, you have the ability to mark important spots such as your campsite, trail-heads, and points of interest. This guarantees you will always be able to return to your original location. Having offline maps for remote regions can be a life-saving resource when limited or no cell service is available. Applications such as Google Maps, AllTrails, and Gaia GPS provide various features for adventurers, including the ability to use them online and offline. These applications also offer up-to-date information, such as trail conditions and user reviews, giving you additional details for your planning.

Utilizing both traditional and digital navigation techniques provides a blend of advantages. Paper maps are dependable in instances of tech-nological failure as they do not require batteries or signals. Always have a physical map of the park with you, even if you intend to rely on a GPS. Looking at information from both sources can boost your overall assurance in exploring the park. Be cautious if your GPS displays a path not found on the map or the map shows a trail not seen on GPS. This repetition guarantees you have all the necessary information, regardless of any obstacles you face.

Incorporating both tools also allows for a more in-depth under-standing of your surroundings. Digital maps can zoom in for detailed views or zoom out for a broader perspective, while paper maps provide a comprehensive overview that's easy to reference at a glance. This dual approach minimizes the risk of getting lost and maximizes your ability to explore confidently. Visualizing your route on a map before you set out can also help you remember landmarks and key turns, making it easier to stay on track.

Understanding how to read and interpret these maps can make your adventures more enjoyable. For example, knowing that a series of closely spaced contour lines indicates a steep ascent can help you prepare mentally and physically for the hike ahead. Recognizing symbols for water sources, rest areas, and scenic viewpoints allows you to plan your breaks and photo ops more effectively. These small details enhance your overall experience, making each outing more enjoyable and less stressful.

GPS technology and applications can simplify navigation by providing instant updates and precise location accuracy. Establish waypoints for where you begin, where you will camp, and any other places you intend to go. Following this method, you can easily return to your starting point, no matter how far you have strayed from the usual route. Having offline maps on hand guarantees you'll always have directions, even in the most isolated locations. Applications such as Google Maps, AllTrails, and Gaia GPS are extremely helpful tools, offering not just navigation but also user feedback, trail status, and places of interest.

Combining traditional and digital navigation tools creates a comprehensive system that adapts to any situation. Paper maps are a reliable backup, ensuring you're never completely lost if your GPS device fails. Comparing information from both sources can highlight discrepancies and provide a fuller picture of the park. This redun- dancy builds confidence, allowing you to explore more freely.

2.3 AVOIDING CROWDS: FINDING HIDDEN GEMS

Seasons significantly impact the availability of parks and the satisfaction of visitors. In winter, parks in northern areas often shut down or provide limited facilities because of snow and low temperatures. Parks in the Midwest and Northeast may close specific trails or areas, reducing crowds but making navigation more difficult. Conversely, spring and summer represent the busiest times of the year. More people are attracted to the warmer weather, resulting in increased crowd levels. California and Carolina's parks experience a high influx of campers, highlighting the importance of making reservations ahead of time. However, visiting during autumn is a great idea. The weather is pleasant, the leaves are transitioning, and the number of people decreases, providing a more peaceful and calm atmosphere. In the autumn, parks in New England are stunning, showcasing colorful leaves and refreshing air.

Each season has unique offerings and activities that can enhance your travel experience. In spring, the lively environment is enriched by the blooming of wildflowers and the movements of birds. The wildflower displays in the parks of the Great Smoky Mountains are well-renowned, making them a perfect destination in the spring. Summer provides increased daylight hours, which are ideal for participating in activities in the water. Parks like those found in Lake Tahoe offer countless chances for water-based fun, like swimming, kayaking, and paddleboarding, thanks to the presence of lakes or rivers. Fall is ideal for exploring foliage and enjoying more pleasant hiking conditions. The stunning autumn colors and scenic overlooks make the Blue Ridge Parkway in Virginia and North Carolina well- known. During the winter, parks remain accessible and offer snow- shoeing, cross-country skiing, and ice fishing, providing a more peaceful experience.

The timing of your visits can significantly impact your experience. Traveling on weekdays rather than weekends can assist in steering clear of large crowds. Most individuals prefer taking short trips on weekends, so if you can plan a mid-week escape, you'll notice the parks are less crowded. Another great tactic is to plan your visit during the shoulder seasons, such as late spring or early fall. You can enjoy favorable weather during these times without the usual peak season crowds. Traveling during non-peak times, avoiding Memorial Day, Fourth of July, and Labor Day, as these vacation dates attract many tourists, leading to difficulties reserving campsites and increasing trail congestion.

Discovering lesser-known parks can provide a quieter and more tranquil experience. Online forums and travel blogs are excellent tools for uncovering secret treasures. Sites like FreeCampsites.net and the Reddit community r/vandwellers frequently post about less popular locations with fewer visitors. Visitor centers in the area provide a lot of value as well. The employees are typically knowledgeable about the region and can suggest secluded parks. Browsing state park websites can uncover lesser-known parks that provide amazing adventures. Instead of the busy Grand Canyon, you could find the peaceful yet equally beautiful Petrified Forest National Park.

Even in popular parks, you can find solitude by exploring underutilized areas. Venturing into the remote sections of the park can lead you to hidden treasures. Less popular trails and campsites often provide a more intimate experience with nature. For example, Yosemite is known for its busy valley, but the high country areas like Tuolumne Meadows are much quieter. Visiting early in the morning or late in the afternoon can also help. Most people hike or sightsee during the middle of the day, so starting your activities early or later can mean fewer people and better light for photography.

Park rangers are an invaluable resource for finding quiet and scenic spots. They know the park inside and out and can provide personal recommendations. Don't hesitate to ask them for tips on less frequented activities or hidden viewpoints. Rangers often know about secret trails or overlooks that aren't on the main maps. Their insights can lead you to some of the park's most beautiful and serene parts, enhancing your overall experience.

2.4 PET-FRIENDLY PARK LISTINGS AND AMENITIES

Discovering the ideal park for you and your four-legged companion can greatly enhance your camping trip. Many state parks allow pets and provide services to ensure their joy and protection. For instance, parks with specified pet zones offer areas where your dog can freely wander, play, and interact with other animals. These regions usually have pet waste stations and water bowls, making maintaining a tidy campsite simple and ensuring your pet stays hydrated. Understanding the rules and regulations regarding pets in state parks is crucial. Certain parks may mandate leashes for pets, while others might impose breed limitations or restrict the number of animals per camp- site. Review the park's website or contact them in advance to confirm you are following their rules.

Many parks provide hiking trails where you can bring your dog to exercise and appreciate nature together. The paths are typically well designated and come in different levels of challenge, allowing you to pick a route that matches your pet's energy and endurance. Another great thing to seek out is beaches and swimming spots that welcome pets. Picture yourself enjoying a sunny day playing fetch in the water or watching your dog have fun splashing around freely. Certain parks also offer designated areas without leashes and specialized spaces for dogs to socialize and exercise freely. These enclosed spaces are ideal for allowing your dog to release some energy in a secure setting.

It is essential to ensure your pet is safe and comfortable while camp- ing. Always make sure to have enough water and pet food for the whole journey, with a bit extra as a precaution. Portable and foldable water bowls provide a practical solution for keeping your pet hydrated while traveling. Offering protection from the sun and covering from the elements is crucial, particularly on sweltering summer days. A pop-up tent or shaded canopy can assist in keeping your pet cool and comfortable. Ensuring that pets are always on a leash and well managed is not just a park requirement but also impor- tant for safety. Keeping your pet under control is crucial due to potential risks from wildlife, other campers, and unfamiliar envi- ronments.

Getting ready for a camping adventure with a pet involves bringing extra supplies. It is crucial to have a pet first aid kit containing bandages, antiseptic wipes, and required medications. Extra leashes and harnesses are handy in case one gets lost or broken. Giving your pet things like beds and toys can help them feel more at ease, reducing stress and improving the travel experience for everyone involved. Don't forget to bring waste bags to pick up messes and a brush to manage shedding.

Some parks exceed expectations with their pet-friendly features. An example is Gulf State Park in Alabama, which includes 28 miles of trails and a dog pond at Lake Shelby and provides pet-friendly geocaching and kayaking activities. There are more than 15 miles of trails at Oracle State Park in Arizona that are suitable for pets, one of which is a part of the Arizona National Scenic Trail. Mendocino Headlands State Park in California is also beautiful, offering dog- friendly trails along the coastline and beaches such as Portuguese Beach and Big River Beach. Every park offers a distinct setting for you and your pet to discover and appreciate.

Camping that allows pets can be a satisfying adventure for you and your four-legged companion. Select parks with appropriate facilities and adhere to basic rules to guarantee your pet a pleasant and secure outing. Having your pet with you while hiking scenic trails, splashing in the water, or relaxing at the campsite enhances the adventure and makes it extra special. Pack your equipment, grab your animal companion, and venture outdoors to discover nature as a team!

2.5   ACCESSIBLE PARKS: CATERING TO ALL ABILITIES

When organizing an RV journey, it's important to take into account accessibility features for individuals with disabilities. Fortunately, numerous state parks are enhancing their efforts to guarantee that the great outdoors is accessible to all. For example, Custer State Park in South Dakota provides restrooms and showers that comply with ADA regulations, which helps travelers with mobility limitations stay comfortable and clean. Not only are there restrooms that are easily accessible, but there are also campsites that are specially made for wheelchairs. These areas typically have smooth grounds paved trails, and are close to necessary facilities, providing a stress-free experience.

Picnic areas and paved trails also cater to those with limited mobility. Parks like Indiana Dunes State Park offer accessible picnic spots with tables designed for wheelchair users and paved paths that wind through scenic landscapes. These features allow everyone to join in on family picnics or enjoy a leisurely stroll through nature without worrying about uneven terrain. Boardwalks over wetlands or around lakes add another accessibility layer, providing safe and stable paths for wheelchairs and strollers.

Accessibility goes beyond ramps and restrooms, encompassing a fully inclusive experience. Spacious, even walkways make it easy for people of all abilities, including wheelchair users and parents with strollers, to move around the park easily. Ramps and handrails assist in important areas such as entryways, bathrooms, and beautiful   views. Accessible parking and transportation choices are equally important. Several parks provide reserved parking spaces near trail entrances and information centers in addition to wheelchair-acces- sible shuttle services. This allows everyone to easily navigate the park without worrying about lengthy, tiring treks from the parking lots.

When planning a trip accommodating all abilities, doing some home-work is essential. Start by checking park websites for detailed accessi-bility information. Many parks provide maps highlighting accessible features and facilities, making it easier to plan your visit. Contacting park offices for specific inquiries can also be incredibly helpful. Park staff are usually well-informed about the latest accessibility updates and can provide personalized advice. Reading reviews from other travelers with disabilities can offer practical insights and tips that official sources might overlook. Websites like AccessNow and

DisabledGo provide user-generated reviews and ratings on accessibility, helping you make informed decisions.

Accessible activities and attractions ensure everyone can enjoy the trip. Multiple parks provide guided tours that consider accessibility, guaranteeing full participation for all individuals. An instance of this is Yellowstone National Park, which offers guided bus tours equipped with wheelchair lifts, allowing all visitors to enjoy the park's renowned geysers and wildlife. Nature centers and educational programs are frequently created with accessibility as a priority, including interactive exhibits at a height suitable for wheelchairs and audio descriptions for those with visual impairments. Scenic drives and viewpoints, which can be reached by car, provide an alternative way to appreciate the park's beauty for those who prefer not to walk a lot. For example, the Blue Ridge Parkway has many lookout points that offer breathtaking views accessible from your car.

By choosing parks with these accessible features, you ensure that everyone in your group can enjoy the trip without unnecessary stress or discomfort. Whether you're exploring paved trails, enjoying a picnic, or taking a scenic drive, accessible parks offer a welcoming environment for travelers of all abilities.

2.6 SAFETY FIRST: CHOOSING SECURE CAMPSITES

Safety should be your top priority when planning an RV trip. Reading reviews and safety ratings is one of the most effective methods to determine the level of safety at a campsite. Campendium and RV Park Reviews provide firsthand experiences from other campers on their websites. Consider feedback on security measures, lighting, and general safety. Examining crime data for the neighborhood can also offer important information. Local police department websites frequently release crime statistics, providing a better understanding of what can be anticipated. Feel free to ask park rangers and staff for advice. They are familiar with the region and can recommend the most secure locations to pitch tents.

Selecting a safe and practical campsite location involves more than   just finding a pretty view. Proximity to park offices and ranger stations can offer an added layer of security. Being close to these facil- ities means help is readily available if you need it. Visibility and acces- sibility are also crucial. A site that's visible from main roads or other campsites is less likely to attract unwanted attention. Avoid low-lying areas prone to flooding, especially if rain is in the forecast. Flooded campsites can quickly turn a relaxing trip into a stressful situation. Look for higher ground, less likely to be affected by sudden weather changes.

Putting in place security measures at campsites can greatly increase your sense of peace. Begin by implementing locks and security systems. Numerous RVs have standard locks, but adding extra secu- rity measures such as wheel locks, hitch locks, and motion sensor lights can offer more protection. Hiding valuable items from view is also a straightforward yet successful tactic. Keep valuable items such as cameras, laptops, and other high-priced products in safe compart- ments or lockboxes. Establishing a camp in brightly lit locations may discourage possible thieves. If there isn't enough lighting on your site, consider using portable lanterns or solar-powered lights. Creating a daily check-in schedule with loved ones can also be a crucial help in times of need. Inform someone of your whereabouts and when you plan to return, allowing them to notify authorities if anything seems wrong.

Preparation for emergencies is essential. Being aware of the nearest medical centers can be very useful in emergencies. Many park visitor centers provide maps and information about nearby hospitals or urgent care facilities. Make sure to have a first aid kit ready with necessary supplies such as gauze, disinfectant wipes, pain medication, and any prescribed medications. Knowing the park's emergency protocols can help you save a significant amount of time. Numerous parks have established guidelines for managing natural disasters, interacting with wildlife, and handling unforeseen situations. There- fore, be sure to review those guidelines once you arrive.

Comprehending these safety measures and putting them into practice can elevate a good trip to a fantastic one. By dedicating time to research and planning, you can fully embrace your adventure without stressing about potential mishaps. Safe camping grounds offer tran- quility and improve the overall camping adventure. Being aware that you are in a secure setting while hiking, fishing, or unwinding by the campfire enables you to enjoy the beauty and peace of nature fully.

As we wrap up this chapter on navigating and finding the perfect campsites, remember that preparation and awareness are your best tools. Whether you understand park layouts, use maps and GPS, discover hidden gems, ensure pet-friendly amenities, or prioritize safety, each step enhances your trip. Now, let's explore the amenities and comforts that make state and county parks feel like home away from home.

CHAPTER 3
AMENITIES AND COMFORTS

I magine this: You have arrived at a state park following a lengthy day of driving. The setting sun sends a warm glow over the trees, and you're eager to reach your campsite finally. Before you can unwind, you must connect your RV. Initially intimidating, the process becomes second nature with some knowledge. Starting with the crucial hookups, let's explore the key steps in setting up your RV campsites.

3.1 HOOKUPS: WATER, ELECTRIC, AND SEWER ESSENTIALS

Having the correct connections is crucial for RV camping. The three primary types are full, partial, and no hookups. Water, electric, and sewer connections are included in full hookups. This arrangement provides maximum convenience, enabling you to utilize your RV's features like yours at your house. Partial hookups typically consist of water and electricity only, providing a relatively comfortable experience, although requiring you to locate a dump station for wastewater disposal. Next is dry camping, also called boondocking, where no utilities are available. This involves detailed planning and effective handling of resources, but it allows for exploring secluded, off-the- grid camping areas.

Accessing a water supply is easy but essential. Begin by employing a water pressure regulator to avoid harm to your RV's plumbing system. After securing the regulator, connect your freshwater hose to the campground's water spigot. Selecting an inline water filter guar- antees clean water delivery to your RV. After establishing the connec- tion, gradually open the tap to inspect for potential leaks and verify everything functions correctly. Start by determining if your RV needs a 30-amp or 50-amp electrical hookup. When connecting it to the power outlet, use a surge protector to protect your electrical system. Plug your RV's power cord into the surge protector and turn on the power. Finally, connect your RV's sewer hose to the outlet and fasten   it with a hose clamp for sewage hookups. Attach the opposite side to the sewage inlet located at the campground. Begin by switching the black water valve to release the waste tank, followed by opening the gray water valve to eliminate any remaining dirt. To prevent contami- nation, switch the order when disconnecting by first dealing with gray water before moving on to black water.

At times, plans don't work out, and that's when troubleshooting is necessary. Insufficient water pressure is a frequently encountered problem. If you encounter this issue, inspect your water pressure regulator to ensure it is properly adjusted. Consider cleaning or replacing your inline water filter. It is essential to have a surge protector for electrical surges or power outages. It can shield your RV from harm and reset itself once power is back. If your sewer hose becomes blocked, use a backflush tool to remove the obstruction. This device attaches to your hose and utilizes the water pressure to clear the blockage, simplifying maintenance.

Saving resources while camping benefits the environment and guarantees all the necessary supplies for your trip. Utilizing LED lights and energy-saving appliances can significantly decrease the amount of electricity you use. These products consume less energy and produce minimal heat, maintaining lower RV temperatures. To save water, think about putting in low-flow fixtures in your RV. These fittings conserve water while maintaining performance, enabling you to extend your water resources. Effective waste disposal is equally important. Utilize environmentally friendly cleaning products and refrain from disposing of chemicals or non-biodegradable items in the sewage system. This ensures the smooth operation of the camp- ground's amenities while also aiding in environmental conservation.

Understanding and using your RV connections can enhance your camping trip for maximum comfort and relaxation. Whether you utilize full hookups for convenience, maximize partial hookups, or opt for dry camping for simplicity, these methods will ensure you're properly prepared for any scenario. Don't hesitate to hook up those hoses and cables and prepare for a peaceful, natural getaway.

3.2 LAUNDRY, SHOWERS, AND DAILY COMFORTS

One of the wonderful aspects of RV camping in state and county parks is the variety of facilities that enhance your stay with comfort and convenience. Several parks provide laundry facilities, which can be a lifesaver during extended journeys. Picture arriving at a campsite after a week of traveling, where you can clean your clothes without the need to search for a laundromat. Search for parks with washing and drying machines that require coins; these are usually located in laundry rooms with folding tables and seats for sitting. Some places also offer detergent and other laundry items for sale to ensure you don't need to worry about bringing your own.

Shower and restroom facilities vary greatly from park to park, but many offer clean, well-maintained options. Private shower stalls provide a bit of luxury and privacy, making your camping experience feel more like a stay at a rustic lodge. Family restrooms are another fantastic feature, especially for those traveling with young children or elderly family members. Hot water availability is usually reliable, but some parks use shower tokens to manage the demand, so it's a good idea to check ahead and be prepared. Cleanliness is always a priority, and most state parks do a commendable job of keeping their facilities in shape.

Daily conveniences extend beyond basic laundry and bathing amenities. Many camping grounds provide picnic tables and fire pits, perfect for enjoying meals outdoors and unwinding by a campfire. Covered areas and shady gazebos provide shade for escaping the sun and are ideal for picnicking or unwinding. The presence of conve- nience stores can offer a wide range of products like snacks, drinks, camping equipment, and souvenirs, which can be highly advanta- geous. These stores nearby allow you to easily find any essential items you may have forgotten without leaving the park.

Achieving optimal comfort while staying involves implementing several practical strategies. Planning out when you will do your laundry and take a shower can have a significant impact. Morning hours or nighttime are usually less busy, giving you the chance to escape the crowds and have a more peaceful experience. Having your preferred soap, shampoo, and a cozy towel with you can help make public showers feel more familiar. Maintaining organization and minimizing clutter is another important factor in ensuring your RV is comfortable. Utilize storage options such as containers and compart-mentalizers to keep items organized. This improves the livability of the space and helps decrease stress when searching for things hurriedly.

Consider creating a short list of vital everyday comfort items to pack. Include a portable fan for hot nights, extra blankets for chilly morn- ings, and a small toolkit for minor repairs. A foldable drying rack can be handy for air-drying clothing and towels outside on nice days. Adding familiar items like a beloved pillow or a warm blanket can enhance your RV's cozy, homey atmosphere.

Consider the small details that can improve your overall experience and physical comfort. Creating a cozy outdoor area with seating, a table, and fairy lights can establish a friendly environment for you and your camping companions. If you like to read, bring some good books and a portable speaker to play music in the background. Adding these little details can transform your campsite into a comfortable sanc- tuary for relaxing after a day of adventure.

Being ready and utilizing the facilities can transform a decent camping experience into an excellent one. Whether washing clothes, having a warm shower, or using on-site amenities, these small luxu- ries contribute to a more pleasant and relaxed experience. Therefore, pack your belongings carefully, schedule your activities, and maxi- mize the facilities available at state and county parks.

3.3 FAMILY-FRIENDLY AMENITIES AND ACTIVITIES

Going on trips with children can be exciting, and discovering family-friendly parks can have a significant impact. Many parks provide amenities for children to enjoy as they unwind. Family-friendly parks typically have playgrounds and play areas as a common feature. These areas prioritize safety, incorporating cushioned flooring and play structures suitable for different age ranges. Tishomingo State Park in

Mississippi offers fantastic playgrounds where children can enjoy climbing, swinging, and sliding to their hearts' delight. Educational activities and programs for kids enhance the enjoyment and knowledge gained. These programs frequently consist of guided nature walks by rangers, junior ranger activities, and interactive experiences that educate children about the environment and wildlife. Family- friendly pools are also popular, offering a secure spot for children to play and refresh during warm weather. Curt Gowdy State Park in Wyoming has pools ideal for family enjoyment, equipped with shallow sections for young kids.

There are numerous activities that the entire family can participate in together. Structured nature hikes and park ranger-led activities provide an excellent opportunity to discover the park's distinct char- acteristics and ecosystem. These strolls are typically simple for people of all ages and offer interesting observations about the surrounding plants and animals. Family fishing locations and instruction can transform a mundane afternoon into a remarkable event. Several parks include lakes or rivers with fish you can teach your children to catch. Picture the thrill of landing their initial catch! Picnic spots equipped with BBQ grills are ideal for enjoying family meals. Parks such as Johnson's Shut-Ins State Park in Missouri provide picturesque areas for picnics, where you can barbecue burgers and have a meal as a group. These locations frequently feature tables, grills, and occa- sionally covered pavilions, making them perfect for family get- togethers.

Ensuring families have a safe and comfortable camping experience requires some advance planning. Ensuring the RV and campsite are childproofed is a positive first step. Protect electrical sockets, fasten loose items, and keep sharp objects from access. It is also important to guarantee safe play spaces. Select camping spots far from bustling roads and provide sufficient room for children to play without risk. Packing essential items for the family can have a significant impact. Remember to bring games, toys, and a fully-equipped first aid kit. Board games and card games are ideal on rainy days, while outdoor toys such as frisbees and balls can provide hours of entertainment for children. It is essential to have a first aid kit containing band-aids, antiseptic wipes, and required medications.

Adding special events and seasonal activities can enhance the magic of your family camping experience. Numerous parks host special events and festivals based on holidays that are popular among children. These activities range from searching for Easter eggs to going door- to-door for Halloween candy. Participating in seasonal crafting classes is also an enjoyable choice. Children can make nature-themed crafts that double as excellent mementos from the journey. Family movie nights and campfire storytelling sessions are great ways to   relax after a day of exciting activities. Parks frequently host movie nights with outdoor screens, providing the opportunity to enjoy family-friendly films while gazing at the stars. Campfire storytelling events unite individuals as rangers or storytellers recount local folk- lore and stories.

Selecting parks with these family-oriented features and things to do guarantees that every family member enjoys themselves. Play areas, educational activities, and pool facilities entertain the children, while guided hikes, fishing trips, and outdoor meals provide enjoyment for the entire family. By taking the necessary precautions and packing the essential items, you can ensure your family camping trip is safe and comfortable. Special occasions and seasonal events bring an addi- tional thrill, forming enduring memories for all. Load up the RV, bring the family together, and prepare for an amazing adventure in the wilderness!

3.4   PET PARKS: DOG-FRIENDLY FACILITIES AND TRAILS

Camping with your furry friend can be a wonderful adventure, but it's crucial to understand the pet regulations at various parks to ensure a smooth journey. Various state and county parks have set down partic- ular rules concerning pets. The majority of parks require dogs to be kept on a leash no longer than six feet. This ensures your pet's safety by protecting them and preventing them from disturbing wildlife or other campers. Checking ahead of time is a smart move to avoid potential problems if your dog isn't one of the breeds typically not allowed in specific parks. Extra fees for animals are frequently neces- sary, too. These fees help cover the maintenance costs of pet-friendly facilities and may range from a nightly charge to a set fee for your entire stay.

One great aspect of parks that welcome pets is the presence of dog parks and areas where dogs can be off-leash. These areas enable your dog to roam and interact with other canines. Enclosed dog parks with agility equipment provide an excellent opportunity for your pet to stay active and mentally engaged. Places such as Four Paws Kingdom Campground in North Carolina are exclusively designed for dogs and offer agility courses and completely enclosed play areas. Open areas and unleashed hiking paths offer dogs increased opportunities to roam and discover. Having access points for dogs to swim in the water is a great extra bene- fit. Picture your dog's joy as it frolics in a lake or river. Waggin' Tail Ranch RV Resort in Texas offers a dog pond that is ideal for dogs.

Campgrounds with amenities that cater to pets enhance the camping experience for both you and your furry companion. Search for parks with pet waste stations and bag dispensers; they simplify cleaning up after your dog and maintaining the cleanliness of the park. Some parks provide pet-friendly accommodations, permitting you to relax without concern for your pet's well-being. Having veterinary services either on- site or close by is also a crucial amenity. Being aware of a nearby veterinarian can offer comfort in case your pet requires medical treatment. Waggin' Tail Ranch RV Resort provides a grooming space for your pet to stay clean and comfortable while you're there.

Keeping your pet safe during your camping trip requires a few precautions. Preventing heatstroke and dehydration is critical, especially in hot weather. Always provide plenty of fresh water and a shaded area where your dog can cool off. Avoid vigorous exercise during the hottest parts of the day. Protecting pets from wildlife and insects is also important. Keep your dog on a leash to prevent encounters with wildlife, and use pet-safe insect repellents to ward off ticks and mosquitoes. Ensuring pets are up-to-date with vaccinations is another key safety measure. Current vaccinations protect your pet from diseases they might encounter in the wild or from other animals.

Camping with pets can be a rewarding experience for both of you. Choosing parks with suitable amenities and following simple guidelines can ensure a safe, comfortable, and fun trip for your furry friend. Whether running free in an off-leash area, splashing in a lake, or relaxing in a pet-friendly cabin, these parks cater to the needs of pets and their owners. So pack up your pet's favorite toys, grab their leash, and head out for an adventure that both you and your furry friend will love!

3.5 PARKS WITH RELIABLE WI-FI AND CELL SERVICE

In the modern era of technology, remaining connected is crucial, especially while enjoying the beauty of nature. Many RV campers depend on dependable internet and cell service. First and foremost, maintaining communication with loved ones is of utmost importance. A strong signal is essential for staying connected while sharing photos, communicating with loved ones, or organizing gatherings during your latest adventure. Reliable internet is essential for remote workers and digital nomads and cannot be compromised. It enables you to work remotely, transforming your RV into a portable workspace. Accessing online resources and emergency services is also crucial. A reliable internet connection is essential for accessing trail maps, checking weather updates, and contacting emergency services, potentially saving lives.

Several parks are known for their strong connectivity, ensuring you stay connected without a hitch. Cape Disappointment State Park in Washington offers high-speed internet access, making it a favorite among digital nomads. The park's unique location, where the Pacific Ocean meets the Columbia River, provides stunning views and reli- able connectivity. Johnson's Shut-Ins State Park in Missouri also   boasts excellent cell service coverage, with maps available for major carriers. This park offers beautiful natural surroundings and ensures you're always in touch. For those needing Wi-Fi hotspots, Lost Dutchman State Park in Arizona provides multiple spots throughout the park, ensuring you can stay connected while enjoying the scenic desert landscape.

Enhancing your connectivity in parks with weaker signals can make a significant difference. Using signal boosters and Wi-Fi extenders can amplify weak signals, providing a more stable connection. These devices are easy to set up and can be a game-changer in areas with spotty coverage. Choosing campsites with better reception is another practical tip. Higher ground or sites closer to the park's entrance often have better signal strength. If all else fails, accessing local libraries or cafes with the internet can provide a temporary solution. Many small towns near state parks have libraries or cafes offering free Wi-Fi, allowing you to catch up on work or stay connected.

Managing data consumption is essential, especially when depending on mobile data for internet usage. Using offline maps and resources can result in a significant reduction in data usage. Apps such as   Google Maps and AllTrails let you save maps for offline use, decreasing the necessity for consistent internet connectivity. Using applications to monitor data usage can assist in tracking the amount of data consumed and preventing additional charges for exceeding limits. Applications such as My Data Manager offer in-depth analysis of your data usage to assist you in staying within your usage limits. Locating complimentary Wi-Fi areas in and near the park can also be beneficial. Numerous visitor centers, campgrounds, and even some scenic viewpoints provide complimentary Wi-Fi, allowing a break from using cellular data.

Considering your internet and cell service requirements can improve your RV camping experience. Staying connected is easier than ever, whether you're posting your travels online, working from a distance, or keeping in touch with family and friends. You have numerous choices available to make sure you are always connected, from parks with good signals to strategies for improving weak connections. Feel free to experience the benefits of both worlds by enjoying nature and staying connected to the digital world.

3.6   NAVIGATING PARKS WITH LARGE RIGS AND SLIDE-OUTS

Navigating large rigs in state and county parks can be a challenge, but it's nothing you can't handle with some preparation. One of the biggest hurdles is maneuverability in tight spaces. Many parks were designed long before RVs grew to their current sizes, and navigating narrow roads or sharp turns can be tricky. Finding campsites that can accommodate larger rigs is another concern. Not all sites are created equal; some might be too short or narrow for your RV. Then there's the issue of managing slide-outs. These can be a blessing for extra space but can easily obstruct neighboring sites if not deployed care- fully. You must ensure ample room on either side of your rig to avoid any inconvenience.

Doing research is important when choosing parks that can accommo- date big rigs. Begin by verifying the measurements of camping areas and entry paths. Several parks provide this information on their websites, or you can contact them in advance for the details. Search for parks that offer pull-through sites, making it simpler for big rigs to maneuver. These sites enable you to enter from one end and exit from the other, removing the necessity for challenging reversing actions. Checking the height clearance is important, especially for taller RVs. Low branches or bridges that are low can be hazardous.

Parks such as Custer State Park in South Dakota are famous for their expansive campsites and broad roads, perfect for accommodating big RVs.

Establishing a big rig efficiently necessitates a touch of finesse. Begin by placing your RV in the best position to maximize space usage. This could involve parking slightly off-center to provide enough space for your slide-outs. After locating the ideal spot, use leveling blocks and stabilizers to guarantee that your RV remains stable and level. This is particularly crucial for big rigs, as irregular terrain can lead to major problems. Ensure that you have sufficient clearance when extending your slide-outs. Walk around your RV and inspect for obstructions like trees, picnic tables, or other vehicles. It's also advisable to talk to your neighbors if you're near their location. A brief conversation can help avoid confusion and guarantee everyone has sufficient room.

Certain parks are very good at accommodating big rigs, which can enhance your stay significantly. Cape Disappointment, State Park in Washington, provides many pull-through sites and spacious access roads, making maneuvering even the biggest vehicles simple. Another great choice is Curt Gowdy State Park in Wyoming, acclaimed for its large camping areas and sufficient room for maneuvering. User feedback frequently mentions parks that excel in providing accommodations for large RVs. Perusing these reviews can offer valuable perspectives and assist in selecting the optimal park for your requirements.

At first, maneuvering through parks with large rigs and slide-outs may seem overwhelming, but it becomes easier to handle with a proper strategy. Through research, choosing suitable parks, and setting up your rig effectively, you can have all the comforts of home while enjoying nature.

CHAPTER 4
ACTIVITIES AND ADVENTURE

A couple of years ago, I was at the entrance of a less popular state park in Oregon, looking at a sign for the "Misery Ridge Trail." Although it had a scary name, I chose to give it a try. As I continued upwards, the scenery's beauty became more awe-inspiring. Reaching the top, I relished a breathtaking vista that justified the hard work and sweat. The beauty of hiking in state and county parks is that every trail provides distinct benefits. There is a trail that will impress you, regardless of whether you are new or skilled at hiking.

4.1 BEST STATE PARKS FOR HIKING TRAILS AND SCENIC VIEWS

Letchworth State Park in New York, often called the "Grand Canyon of the East," offers some of the most spectacular hiking trails. With 66 miles of trails to choose from, you'll find something for every skill level. The Gorge Trail is a must-do, featuring stunning views of the three major waterfalls and the Genesee River. It's about 7 miles one way and moderately difficult. Spring and fall are the best times to hike here, as the weather is mild and the foliage is either blooming or turning vibrant shades of red and gold.

Another popular spot in Pennsylvania is Ricketts Glen State Park, known for its seven-mile Falls Trail, which features 21 named waterfalls. This path is rugged, steep, and rocky, but the reward is worthwhile. The waterfalls come in different sizes and levels of beauty, providing a scenic opportunity ideal for photography lovers. Summer is the perfect season for hiking this trail, as the water flow is highest, and the forest is vibrant and green.

For a truly one-of-a-kind experience, check out the coastal trails in Anza-Borrego Desert State Park in California. It is California's biggest state park, covering 585,930 acres of mountains, slot canyons, and wildflower meadows. The Borrego Palm Canyon Trail is well- liked, taking you through desert scenery to a secret cluster of palm trees and a tiny waterfall. The trail spans around 3 miles in total and is of medium difficulty. Spring is the optimal time to see the desert floor covered in wildflowers, forming a colorful tapestry.

Tallulah Gorge State Park in Georgia provides the Gorge Floor Trail for history enthusiasts, leading them down 100 feet to Hurricane Falls' base. This particular path is tough, needing a permit and some scrambling, but the sights of the waterfalls and the gorge are truly unforgettable. The fall foliage enhances the stunning scenery, making autumn the ideal time for hiking in this area.

Safety is crucial when hiking; taking simple precautions can greatly enhance your adventure. Always be ready for any changes in the weather. Despite clear forecasts, conditions can change quickly, especially in mountainous regions. Bring clothing for all types of weather, including rain gear and sun protection. Having the right equipment and supplies is essential. Essentials for hiking include good boots, a backpack with water, snacks, a first aid kit, and a map or GPS. It is crucial to also remain on designated paths. Deviation from the path can lead to getting lost; marked trails ensure safety and environmental protection.

Access is crucial for all individuals to appreciate the charm of state parks. Numerous parks provide smooth, flat trails for individuals of all skill levels. For instance, Mount Tamalpais State Park in California provides numerous wheelchair-friendly paths that offer breathtaking scenery of the Bay Area and the Golden Gate Bridge. Many of these pathways have spots for resting and seating, allowing for leisurely breaks amidst the beautiful views. If you struggle with mobility or just like an easier hike, these accessible trails ensure everyone can enjoy the outdoors.

Numerous hiking trails are just waiting to be discovered, from the challenging paths in Letchworth State Park to the seaside routes in Anza-Borrego. Tie your hiking boots, prepare your backpack, and embark on a journey that guarantees stunning scenery and lasting memories. Enjoy your hike!

4.2   FISHING SPOTS AND REGULATIONS

When it comes to fishing, state and county parks offer some of the best spots you can find. Take Lake Ouachita in Arkansas—it's a prime location for largemouth bass, walleye, and catfish. The lake is stocked regularly, ensuring a plentiful supply of fish for both seasoned anglers and beginners. If you're into fly fishing, the White River in Arkansas is renowned for its trout population. The river's clear, cold waters are perfect for catching rainbow and brown trout, making it a go-to spot for fly fishing enthusiasts. For a quieter experience, consider the Little Red River, also in Arkansas. This river is known for its serene envi- ronment and is perfect for beginners who want to practice their skills without the pressure of crowded fishing spots.

You cannot overlook fishing regulations. Typically, you must obtain a fishing license from state parks; this can be done online or at nearby stores. Catch limits and seasonal restrictions are frequently imple- mented to maintain the health of fish populations. In numerous loca- tions, there are restrictions on how many fish you can catch each day, and some species are protected during their breeding season. Different parks have different rules on fishing techniques; some allow bait and tackle, while others limit you to fly fishing. Make sure to review the park's specific regulations to prevent incurring fines or penalties during your visit.

Next, let's discuss strategies for ensuring a successful fishing excur- sion. Having the correct bait and tackle can greatly impact the outcome. Plastic worms and crankbaits are commonly suggested for bass fishing. If your goal is to catch trout, consider using live bait such as worms or artificial lures. The optimal times for fishing are typically in the early morning and late afternoon when fish are most lively. Different methods may be used based on the specific kind of fish you are trying to catch. Bottom fishing with stink bait can be highly successful when targeting catfish, as an illustration. In contrast, trout fly fishing needs finesse, with lightweight lures mimicking surface- skimming insects.

Family-friendly fishing locations are a fantastic way to introduce children to the pleasures of fishing. Locations such as Lake Eufaula in Alabama are ideal for family excursions. The lake is filled with blue catfish and bass, with picnic areas and restrooms nearby for families' convenience. Convenient access is essential when fishing with children. Search for spots near the water to park, minimizing the gear you need to transport. Safety considerations are of utmost impor- tance. Make sure that young anglers always wear life jackets, particu- larly when fishing from a boat or close to deep water. Educating children about fishing fundamentals, such as casting and reeling, can provide an enjoyable and instructional opportunity.

Fishing in state and county parks offers more than just a hobby; it allows for a connection with nature and the making of lasting memo- ries. Fishing in a well-stocked lake, peaceful river, or tranquil pond can be enjoyed by anyone due to the excitement of catching fish. Having the appropriate understanding of rules, strategies, and places suitable for families, you are on track for a prosperous fishing trip. Therefore, prepare your equipment, obtain your fishing permit, and make your way to one of these amazing spots for a day of leisure and thrills by the water.

4.3 BIRD WATCHING AND WILDLIFE OBSERVATION

On a chilly morning, I was at Kenai Fjords National Park in Alaska, using binoculars to observe the different bird species native to the area. This park is a perfect place for bird enthusiasts, with around 200 different bird species, such as puffins, murres, and bald eagles often seen. Various locations throughout the country provide excellent chances to see a diverse array of bird species because of the high number of migrating populations. Dauphin Island in Alabama is also a treasure, with more than 400 bird species migrating through its coastal pine forests, wetlands, and sand dunes. In the spring and fall migrations, the island is busy with bird activity, making it ideal for bird watchers of all skill levels.

Wetlands and marshes provide abundant opportunities for bird-watching. Delaware's Bombay Hook National Wildlife Refuge covers almost 16,000 acres and houses hundreds of thousands of snow geese during the winter. A broad range of birds, such as shorebirds, water-fowl, and raptors, are drawn to the different habitats found in this area. Forests with unique bird species offer a distinctive type of excitement. The Chiricahua Mountains in Arizona are renowned for hosting 13 different kinds of hummingbirds, resulting in a lively and colorful display. Exploring these wooded regions could also lead you to encounter other uncommon species, such as the graceful trogon or the Montezuma quail.

For a better wildlife viewing experience, follow these critical, safe, and responsible observation guidelines. Binoculars and spotting scopes are essential instruments. They enable you to observe animals up close without causing any disturbance, whether observing a faraway eagle or a group of deer. Maintaining a crucial safe distance is important. It not only guarantees your safety, but it also reduces stress on the animals. Follow the general guideline: if your thumb can hide the animal when held at arm's length, you are at a safe distance. Wildlife sightings are most common during early mornings and late afternoons when animals are typically more active. Weather condi- tions can also influence wildlife activity, with cooler, overcast days typically leading to more animal sightings.

State parks are teeming with a variety of species. Birds of prey, like hawks and eagles, are common in many parks. For instance, the Morley Nelson Snake River Birds of Prey National Conservation Area in Idaho boasts North America's highest density of nesting raptors. Songbirds and waterfowl are also abundant, especially in wetlands and forested areas. Mammals like deer, elk, and bears roam freely in parks like Glacier National Park in Montana. Reptiles and amphibians inhabit specific habitats, like the wetlands of Ash Meadows National Wildlife Refuge in Nevada, home to various lizards, snakes, and frogs.

Participating in citizen science initiatives can add a fulfilling dimen- sion to wildlife observation activities. Reporting sightings to local wildlife organizations helps scientists track and protect species. Many parks offer bird counts and surveys, where volunteers can contribute valuable data. These events are often fun and educational, providing a deeper understanding of the local ecosystem. You can also use wildlife observation apps like eBird or iNaturalist to log your sightings. These apps keep track of your observations and contribute to larger conser- vation efforts by sharing data with researchers.

Whether you're an experienced birder or just starting out, the thrill of spotting a rare bird or observing wildlife in their natural habitat is unparalleled. With the right tools, a bit of knowledge, and a commit- ment to responsible observation, you can enjoy some of the best bird- watching and wildlife experiences state and county parks have to offer.

4.4   SCENIC DRIVES AND OVERLOOKS

Imagine cruising through the rolling hills of Shenandoah National Park in Virginia, with the Blue Ridge Mountains stretching before you. Skyline Drive is a route that offers panoramic views at every   turn. Starting at the Front Royal Entrance, this 105-mile drive takes   you through diverse landscapes, from lush forests to open meadows. Along the way, you'll find plenty of scenic overlooks where you can pull over and soak in the vistas. Whether it's spring blooms or fall foliage, this drive never disappoints.

Another incredible drive is the Coastal Drive in Redwood National and State Parks, California. Here, you'll navigate towering redwood groves along rugged coastlines and past serene prairies. The nine-mile stretch offers stunning views of the Pacific Ocean and the Klamath River estuary. Seasonal changes add a new layer of beauty, with spring bringing vibrant wildflowers and autumn offering a golden hue to the landscape. Enderts Beach Road provides a perfect spot to park and explore the coastline on foot, making it a versatile option for drivers and hikers.

Signal Mountain Summit Road in Grand Teton National Park, Wyoming, is a must-visit for enthusiasts of high-altitude expeditions. This route leads to one of the park's tallest peaks, providing wide-reaching views of the Teton Range and Jackson Hole Valley. The path is especially stunning in autumn when the aspen trees change to a bright yellow color. All visitors can easily access the overlooks here, allowing everyone to appreciate the beautiful views. Schedule your trip for either early morning or late afternoon to take advantage of optimal lighting and avoid large crowds.

Taking photos of these picturesque drives can result in a rewarding experience. The best times to take photos are early morning and late afternoon, when the gentle light brings out colors and minimizes harsh shadows. Utilizing various lenses can also have a significant impact. A broad-angle lens is excellent for capturing vast landscapes, whereas a telephoto lens can zoom in on faraway details. When framing your photos, keep in mind the rule of thirds. Position the horizon line on either the top or bottom third of the frame for a well- composed and captivating photograph. Remember to try out various angles and viewpoints to diversify your photos.

Preparing for your scenic drive requires some planning. Begin by making sure to review the state of the roads and the upcoming weather predictions in order to prevent unexpected situations. Verifi- cation is recommended as certain routes may be closed in specific seasons. Getting your vehicle ready is very important, especially for extended journeys. Ensure your gas tank is completely filled, and inspect your tires and fluids. Bringing along snacks and supplies can enhance the enjoyment of the trip. Make sure to pack a lot of water, some convenient snacks, and a cooler filled with beverages. Making a driving playlist can also improve the overall experience. Select music that enhances the surroundings and creates the right atmosphere for your journey.

Adding a few stops along the way can make your drive even more memorable. Look for points of interest like historical markers, small towns, or unique natural features. These stops not only break up the drive but also offer new opportunities for exploration. For instance, on the Crater Lake Rim Drive in Oregon, you can stop at the various overlooks to marvel at the deepest lake in the U.S. Trolley tours are available in the summer, providing a guided experience with plenty of photo opportunities.

Appreciating a picturesque car ride involves more than just reaching the final destination; it's also about the actual journey. By properly organizing your trip, you can take full advantage of these beautiful paths and build unforgettable experiences. Load your car, take your camera, and embark on a memorable journey.

4.5   WATER ACTIVITIES: SWIMMING, BOATING, AND KAYAKING

Picture diving into a state park lake with the sun shining brightly and crystal-clear water. Swimming in specified locations can provide a rejuvenating way to beat the heat, especially in the warm summer season. Many state parks have specific swimming spots and beaches that are great for a family day out or a relaxing swim. These areas frequently include safety measures such as lifeguards and designated swimming areas with buoys to protect everyone's safety. In Nevada's Lake Tahoe State Park, you can enjoy lovely sandy beaches with life-guards on duty during the busiest times. Before going out, always verify the water quality and seasonal conditions. It is essential to be informed as certain parks may have warnings about algae blooms or other temporary problems.

Boating provides a fresh perspective on enjoying the water. State parks frequently offer a range of boating options, including renting a rowboat or bringing your own motorboat. Numerous parks provide boat rental opportunities, including canoes, kayaks, paddleboards, and motorboats. At Lake Havasu State Park in Arizona, you can rent a paddleboard to discover the peaceful coves of the lake. There are many locations for canoeing and paddleboarding, with tranquil waters ideal for a relaxing paddle. You can also enjoy motor boating and water skiing if you want more excitement. Parks such as Lake Murray State Park in Oklahoma offer specific areas for high-speed water activities, guaranteeing an exciting experience on the water.

Exploring new places in state parks through kayaking can lead you to the most beautiful and peaceful areas. Novices may enjoy peaceful lakes, where they can paddle and become acquainted with the kayak. Mirror Lake State Park in Wisconsin provides calm, smooth waters perfect for beginners; for individuals with some extra knowledge, rivers, and streams offer a slightly greater level of difficulty. The Buffalo National River in Arkansas is a great location for skilled kayak- ers, thanks to its meandering waters and intermittent rapids. Scenic paths with chances to see wildlife provide an additional level of thrill. Picture gliding through a peaceful inlet, observing herons, turtles, and possibly a river otter. Everglades National Park in Florida provides guided kayak tours showcasing the area's wildlife and ecosystem.

Safety should always come first when participating in water sports and activities. Wearing life jackets and other safety gear is absolutely essential and cannot be debated. A life jacket can still be a lifesaver for experienced swimmers in unforeseen circumstances. Another critical step is to assess weather and water conditions before going out. Unexpected storms or fluctuations in water levels can lead to hazardous situations. Several parks offer live updates on their websites or at visitor centers. Adhering to park regulations is impor- tant for your safety and for protecting the natural environment. Certain activities are only permitted in designated areas within some parks; therefore, always ensure you are in the appropriate zone.

Discovering swimming areas, boating opportunities, and kayaking experiences at state parks can completely immerse you in the beauty and peace of nature. Activities such as diving into a cool lake, paddling through calm waters, or navigating a winding river provide a special opportunity to connect with nature. Grab your swimwear,   life vest, and adventurous spirit, and immerse yourself in the aquatic activities at state parks.

4.6   SEASONAL EVENTS AND LOCAL ATTRACTIONS

Spring in state parks is a wondrous season filled with vibrant colors and abundant life. Many parks host gatherings that honor wildflow- ers, allowing individuals to admire the wide variety of colors present in the natural world. Anza-Borrego Desert, State Park in California, showcases a colorful blanket of vibrant wildflowers that completely change the appearance of the desert. Festivals frequently include nature walks led by knowledgeable guides to teach you about various species. Another intriguing aspect of spring is the migration of birds and their movement. Magee Marsh Wildlife Area is famous among bird enthusiasts in Ohio due to the large population of migrating birds that frequent the area. Witnessing wildlife in its natural habitat, such as elk calving in Rocky Mountain National Park, offers special opportunities to observe animals. Many spring break options, such as craft classes and scavenger hunts, are available for families to enter- tain and engage children.

Summer increases the thrill with a mix of events and activities that attract tourists to state parks. Outdoor concerts and festivals are incredibly popular, providing live music set against beautiful back- drops of landscapes. Parks such as Tanglewood in Massachusetts hold summer concert series that draw music enthusiasts worldwide. Ranger- led programs and educational workshops offer a more in- depth knowledge of the park's ecosystem. These programs frequently involve practical activities such as fossil excavations, night sky obser- vations, and tracking wildlife. Water sports and beach activities define summer. Numerous parks provide designated swimming zones, boat rentals, and spots for paddleboarding. For example, Lake Tahoe State

Park offers various water activities like jet skiing and kayaking, catering to a wide range of interests.

Autumn transforms state parks with colorful leaves and lower temperatures, creating a unique beauty. Fall foliage tours and scenic drives are essential due to their stunning views of the vibrant leaves during the fall season. National parks such as the Great Smoky Mountains National Park offer guided tours showcasing the top locations for admiring autumn foliage. Harvest festivals and community fairs contribute a celebratory vibe to the parks. These occurrences frequently include regional goods, handmade items, and live performances, providing a fantastic opportunity to immerse yourself in the local culture. Observing wildlife during rutting and migration seasons presents one-of-a-kind opportunities for observation. During Elk rutting season in areas such as Yellowstone National Park, it is a magnificent sight to see bulls showcasing their antlers and participating in intense battles. Birds are still migrating, with various species moving through, providing an excellent bird-watching opportunity.

During winter, state parks become magical with snow and ice, providing various activities that make the cold enjoyable. Holiday light shows and winter festivals create a festive atmosphere in the parks. The Garden of Lights at Brookside Gardens in Maryland is an impressive attraction that attracts visitors from all over. Snowshoe- ing, cross-country skiing, and sledding are well-liked winter pastimes. Parks such as Custer State Park in South Dakota provide groomed trails for skiing, snowshoeing, and designated sledding hills for enjoy- ment with family. Observing and tracking wildlife in the winter offers a unique view of the park's resident animals. Footprints in the snow help locate animals such as deer, foxes, and even wolves. Certain   parks provide guided tracking tours, where skilled rangers instruct visitors on recognizing various tracks and indicators of wildlife presence.

Seasonal happenings and nearby points of interest enhance the state park visit, providing options for all visitors regardless of the season.

Each season has its distinct allure, from the colorful flowers in spring to the festive events in summer, the changing foliage in fall, and the peaceful beauty in winter. These activities improve your experience and form enduring recollections, turning each visit to a state park into a fresh journey. Therefore, whether observing the spring migra- tion, attending a summer concert, admiring autumn foliage, or discovering a winter wonderland, state parks always have something unique in store for you.

CHAPTER 5

ECO-FRIENDLY CAMPING

W hile camping one evening at a secluded state park in Maine, I was mesmerized by the unspoiled beauty of the environ- ment. The air was cool, the stars were shining, and the only noises were the rustling leaves and far-off owl hoots. It was a flawless moment of being in sync with the natural world. However, I pondered how long these pristine landscapes would exist if we failed to safeguard them. That evening, I understood the significance of environmentally conscious camping and our responsibility to protect these natural gems.

5.1 LEAVE NO TRACE PRINCIPLES

The Leave No Trace principles are fundamental to sustainable camping. They show us ways to reduce our environmental impact. These principles are guidelines and beliefs that guide our interaction with nature to safeguard it for future generations. Let's explore these seven principles and learn how to utilize them in your RV camping experiences.

Initially, anticipate and prepare. Effective planning guarantees your security and reduces environmental harm. Before you travel to your destination, look into any specific rules or recommendations. Be informed about the weather, bring the appropriate equipment, and book accommodations in advance if necessary. For example, being aware of the requirement to only camp in specified areas at a park can prevent any rushed decisions and ensure that you comply with the regulations.

Afterward, journey and set up your campsite on surfaces that will not easily get damaged. This involves following designated paths and campsites to prevent harm to the environment. Venturing off the designated path can damage plants and disrupt wildlife homes. Long-lasting surfaces are gravel, rock, sand, and established paths. When camping, opt for an established campsite instead of making a new one. This action assists in safeguarding delicate ecosystems that may require many years to heal from even minor disruptions.

Properly getting rid of waste is a principle that we must all embrace. Remove all garbage, uneaten food, and debris. This is not only about how things look; it's about safeguarding animals and preserving the ecosystem's natural equilibrium. Animals can become ill or perish from ingesting human food or garbage. Remember to bring trash bags and take everything you brought when you leave. This refers to easily decomposable waste, such as banana peels or apple cores, which may appear innocuous but potentially disturb wildlife patterns in the area.

Do not take anything you discover. This principle focuses on maintaining the original natural and historical character of the destina- tions you explore. Do not give in to the temptation to pluck flowers, gather rocks, or disrupt any natural or historical items. These compo- nents are integral to the ecosystem, and each has specific functions to fulfill. Collecting rocks or plants may appear unimportant, but the effect can be significant when done by numerous visitors. Appreciate the beauty of these items, snap some photos, but remember to leave them for others to enjoy.

Reduce the negative effects of campfires. Although campfires are a treasured aspect of camping, they have the potential to cause signifi- cant damage if not managed correctly. Utilize a portable stove for cooking and appreciate the illumination of a candle lantern. If a fire is necessary, utilize existing fire rings, fire pans, or mound fires. Main- tain a small fire and only use small sticks found on the ground for burning. Always ensure that a fire is never left unattended, and make sure it is fully extinguished before leaving. Soak the ashes with water, mix them, and soak them once more until they cool down.

Show consideration for the animals in their natural habitat. Watching animals in their natural habitat while camping is a wonderful experi- ence, but it is important to maintain a safe distance. Do not come near, give food to, or bother animals. Providing food to wild animals can cause them to rely on humans and alter their natural actions. Utilize binoculars or a zoom lens to observe from a closer distance without invading their privacy. Protecting your food and garbage is vital to avoid animals accessing it, which could harm them and lead to risky situations.

In conclusion, remember to be thoughtful towards other guests. Nature is accessible to all individuals, and being thoughtful improves the overall experience for everyone. Maintain low noise levels, give way to fellow hikers, and be considerate of the privacy of other campers. Make sure to manage your pets and pick up after them if you decide to bring them along. Showing consideration ensures that   all individuals can experience the peace and loveliness of nature.

To bring these principles to life, let's look at specific examples of how you can implement them in your RV camping. Start by using established campsites whenever possible. These sites are designed to minimize environmental impact and often have amenities like fire rings and picnic tables. Packing out all trash and waste is easier if you bring along dedicated trash bags and plan for waste disposal. Avoid picking plants or disturbing natural features by teaching your children the importance of observation without disruption. Make it a game to see who can spot the most interesting natural feature without touching it.

Sharing the Leave No Trace principles with others is a powerful way to spread awareness and promote eco-friendly practices. Use social media to share your experiences and tips. Educate your children and family members about these principles through hands-on activities. Participate in Leave No Trace training programs to deepen your understanding and become an advocate for responsible outdoor   ethics.

There are many success stories related to implementing Leave No Trace practices. Campers who adhere to these principles are respon- sible for keeping campgrounds in pristine condition, such as those in the Adirondacks. Park rangers frequently tell stories about the posi- tive impact of Leave No Trace methods on restoring natural habitats and safeguarding animals. Regenerated natural spaces, like the tree- planting projects in numerous state parks, demonstrate the beneficial outcomes of such processes.

Adopting the Leave No Trace guidelines goes beyond simply obeying a list of rules; it involves nurturing a profound reverence for the envi- ronment and guaranteeing the preservation of these pristine locations for our descendants. Whether you're a seasoned RVer or a novice camper, these guidelines provide a roadmap to responsible and fulfilling outdoor experiences.

5.2   MANAGING WASTE: GRAY WATER AND BLACK WATER

Knowing the distinctions between gray and black water is essential for RVers who want to camp responsibly. Gray water is the somewhat clean wastewater generated from sinks and showers. While it could have soap and food bits, it is not as dangerous as black water. Wastewater from toilets is known as black water. This particular waste includes human waste and is significantly more dangerous, necessitating meticulous disposal to avoid contamination and health hazards.

There is no room for negotiation regarding the correct disposal of gray and black water. Make sure always to utilize designated dumping areas to empty your tanks. These stations are specially created to manage the waste in a safe manner and avoid causing contamination to the environment. Before beginning, acquaint yourself with the park's rules and instructions. Numerous parks have designated hours for the dump station's availability, with possible additional regula- tions on the chemicals permitted for tank use. Illegal dumping is detrimental to the environment and against the law and can lead to significant penalties. Make sure your hoses are properly attached at all times to avoid any potential spills or leaks.

Reducing the amount of gray and black water you generate can make your camping experience more eco-friendly. One effective way is to use water-saving fixtures and appliances. Install low-flow shower- heads and faucets to cut down on water use. Taking shorter showers and turning off the water while you lather up can also make a big difference. Using biodegradable soaps and detergents helps reduce the chemical load in your gray water, making it less environmentally harmful. These small changes can significantly reduce water usage and the frequency you need to empty your tanks.

The environmental impact of improper waste disposal is severe. Contaminating water sources can have dire consequences for both wildlife and human communities. When black water isn't disposed of properly, it can seep into groundwater or run off into rivers and lakes. This contamination can harm aquatic life and make the water unsafe for drinking and recreational activities. Improper disposal can also harm plant life, as the chemicals and waste products can disrupt soil health and damage vegetation. Over time, these effects can lead to the degradation of natural habitats, making them less hospitable for wildlife and less enjoyable for future campers.

You can reduce your environmental footprint by recognizing the distinctions between gray and black water and following the correct disposal procedures. Using environmentally friendly soaps and detergents in your RV decreases the amount of chemicals in your gray water and simplifies its maintenance. Thoroughly wash your hoses and connections while at the dump station. This method prevents the accumulation of deposits that may result in blockages and leaks. Adhering to park rules and guidelines helps preserve the environment and show respect for regulations that maintain accessibility and enjoyment of these stunning sites for all.

Reducing waste is a continuous process that necessitates deliberate choices and minor changes.

Using dishes and utensils that can be washed and used again reduces the amount of waste from disposable items. When you cook, think about using just one pot to make food, which will lessen the amount of dishes you have to clean. Save excess water from cooking or washing dishes in a receptacle for future use, like flushing the toilet or washing gear. Every small contribution is valuable, and these minor adjustments can significantly decrease your total waste impact.

Many campers may find motivation in understanding the environmental consequences of inappropriate waste disposal. Witnessing the impact of waste on environments and water sources may motivate you to choose more sustainable options. If you happen upon a tainted water source while traveling, it can be a strong reminder of the signif-icance of waste management. Sharing these experiences with fellow campers can increase awareness and motivate others to embrace better practices.

Following these actions safeguards the environment and improves your camping adventure. Once you are sure you are handling your waste properly, you can concentrate on appreciating the beauty and peace of nature. Knowing that you're helping preserve these locations can enhance the enjoyment of hiking, fishing, and camping. There- fore, when you go out in your RV again, remember these tips for handling gray and black water and have a worry-free trip.

5.3 ECO-FRIENDLY PRODUCTS AND PRACTICES

Using the correct items can have a significant impact on eco-conscious RV camping. We will begin with eco-friendly cleaning products. These items decompose organically and have no negative impact on the environment. Companies such as Seventh Generation provide a variety of eco-friendly soaps, detergents, and cleaning prod-ucts that are efficient and environmentally safe. These items are devoid of toxic substances and are secure for use near children and animals, which makes them ideal for family camping excursions. Transitioning to biodegradable alternatives lessens your environ- mental footprint and guarantees you aren't creating harmful waste.

Next up, reusable containers and utensils are a no-brainer. Plastic waste is one of the most significant environmental issues we face, and using reusable items is a simple way to cut down on this. Invest in stainless steel water bottles, silicone food storage bags, and bamboo cutlery. These products are durable, easy to clean, and can be used repeatedly. Bringing your reusable containers for leftovers or snacks also helps you avoid single-use plastics. Not only does this reduce waste, but it also saves you money in the long run.

Solar-powered gadgets and chargers are another fantastic addition to your eco-friendly camping toolkit. These devices harness the sun's power to charge your electronics without relying on fossil fuels.

Products like solar-powered lanterns, phone chargers, and portable solar panels can make your camping experience more sustainable. They're especially useful for boondocking or dry camping, where you might not have access to traditional power sources. They're quiet and don't produce emissions, making them a greener alternative to gas-powered generators.

Using environmentally friendly products is equally crucial as implementing sustainable camping methods. Minimizing the use of disposable plastics is an important move. Choose products with minimal packaging, and remember to bring reusable bags for any items you might need to purchase. Opting for organic and locally sourced food helps local farmers and decreases the carbon footprint from long-distance food transportation. Search for nearby farmers' markets or local co-ops near where you will be camping. Implementing energy- saving measures is another crucial component. Switch off lights and electronic devices when unused, and opt for energy-saving bulbs and appliances. Minor adjustments such as these can significantly decrease your total energy usage.

Do-it-yourself solutions can also significantly impact increasing the sustainability of your camping adventure. For instance, creating your own natural insect repellents at home is simple and works just as well as insect repellents sold in stores. A basic blend of citronella, eucalyptus, and lavender essential oils with a carrier oil can naturally repel bugs without solid chemicals. Creating your own composting toilets is also a fantastic DIY project. Setting them up is surprisingly simple and can greatly reduce water consumption. Utilizing sawdust or coconut coir as a covering material aids in decomposing waste and managing odors. Creating homemade cloth wipes from old t-shirts or towels is also a simple DIY task. They are ideal for cleaning spills or wiping surfaces and are machine washable for multiple uses.

When discussing environmentally conscious brands, multiple ones are notable for their dedication to sustainable practices. Patagonia is famous for its environmentally friendly equipment. They incorporate recycled materials into their products and are dedicated to fair labor practices. Their equipment is sturdy and built to be long-lasting, decreasing the necessity for frequent changes. BioLite is a brand that deserves to be noted. They provide various environmentally friendly energy products such as stoves and solar panels ideal for camping. Their items are created with efficiency and environmental conscious- ness, appealing to campers who care about the environment. As previ- ously stated, Seventh Generation is at the forefront of eco-friendly cleaning products. Their items are made from plants, free from animal cruelty, and come in recycled packaging, which makes them a popular option for environmentally friendly cleaning.

Incorporating eco-friendly products and techniques into your RV camping regimen can be easy. You can reduce your environmental impact significantly by making thoughtful choices and doing simple DIY projects. Using eco-friendly cleaning products, cutting down on disposable plastics, or harnessing solar power can have a beneficial effect. By supporting eco-friendly brands, you contribute to advancing sustainability efforts. When embarking on your next road trip, remember these tips to ensure your camping excursion is as environmentally friendly as possible.

5.4 SOLAR POWER AND RENEWABLE ENERGY OPTIONS

Picture yourself parking your RV in a secluded, serene state park, far from the closest campground. Solar panels silently produce the energy required to power your devices and illuminate your space while the sun shines. Decreasing dependency on fossil fuels is one of the greatest advantages of utilizing solar energy. Solar power is abun- dant and clean, using a sustainable source in nearly every location where the sun is present. This implies that you can camp in remote areas without the need to search for an electrical connection or operate a loud generator. Over time, you will also witness substantial financial savings. Although the upfront cost of solar panels and associated gear may be high, the lasting advantages include decreased energy expenses, fewer refueling visits, and the added perk of shrinking your carbon footprint. Solar power generation is silent, in contrast to standard generators, enabling you to appreciate the peaceful sounds of nature without any disturbances.

Establishing a solar energy system for your motorhome requires a couple of essential tasks. To begin with, it is important to select the appropriate solar panels. Portable RV solar panels offer a convenient solution for those seeking a simple setup that is also easy to transport. They usually come in panels with a power rating of 100 watts and are ideal for small power requirements such as charging devices and powering lights. A permanent solar panel system could be the best option if you need extra energy. These systems are pricier but highly effective, optimizing the rooftop area of your RV for increased energy production, perfect for powering appliances such as refrigerators, microwaves, and air conditioners. After selecting your panels, you must set up charge controllers and inverters. The charge controller regulates the transfer of power from the panels to the batteries to avoid overcharging or discharging. The inverter changes the direct current from the solar panels into alternating current for your RV's consumption. Determining your energy requirements and storage capabilities is essential. Create a list of the devices you intend to supply power to and remember to include their wattage. Utilize cautious assumptions regarding the performance of solar panels, like producing 350 watts daily for each 100-watt panel, to guarantee sufficient capacity.

Although solar power is excellent, other renewable energy choices exist. Wind turbines can be valuable to RVs, especially when frequenting windy campsites. These portable turbines can produce energy round-the-clock, enhancing your existing solar power system. Setting them up is simple and can be installed on your RV or a nearby stand. Portable hydro generators present another appealing choice, especially for those who frequently camp close to running water. These devices harness the power of flowing water's kinetic energy to produce electricity, offering a dependable energy source as long as the water moves. Bioenergy options, like biogas generators, can also be successful. These systems transform organic waste into energy that can be used, providing a sustainable solution for those with high levels of organic waste production. They are harder to install but provide a distinctive method for producing energy while minimizing waste.

Real-life instances and stories of accomplishment demonstrate the advantages of incorporating sustainable energy solutions for RV camping. For example, consider Sarah, a full-time RVer, who discussed her transition to solar energy. Since installing a permanent solar panel system on her RV's roof, she has never regretted her deci- sion. The system provides electricity for her lights, refrigerator, laptop, and phone chargers. Sarah enjoys the freedom of camping in remote areas without the need to search for an electrical connection. One more instance involves a pair that made investments in solar panels and a wind turbine. Camping in uncertain weather conditions is standard, so having dual power sources guarantees a constant and dependable energy supply. It has been discovered that the wind turbine functions very effectively during nighttime or overcast days when solar panels are not as efficient.

Cost-benefit analyses of renewable energy investments often show that while the initial setup can be pricey, the long-term savings are substantial. For example, one RVer calculated that their solar panel system paid for itself in under three years, thanks to the savings on generator fuel and campground hookup fees. They also noted the added benefit of fewer maintenance issues than traditional genera- tors, which can be prone to breakdowns and require regular servicing. Another camper who installed a portable hydro generator found that it provided a reliable power source during their stays near rivers and significantly reduced their overall energy costs. They appreciated sustainability, knowing they were using a renewable resource that didn't harm the environment.

Integrating renewable energy solutions such as solar panels, wind turbines, and hydro generators into your RV camping setup provides several advantages. You will experience the flexibility to camp without being connected to utilities, save money in the long run, and lessen your environmental footprint. Additionally, the silent and eco- friendly energy production enables you to thoroughly engage in the peace and serenity of the environment without the continual noise of a generator. Whether experienced in RVing or new to it, considering these sustainable energy choices can improve your camping trip and support the conservation of the landscapes you cherish.

5.5 SUPPORTING CONSERVATION EFFORTS

In the beauty of nature, it's easy to forget that these landscapes need our help to stay pristine. Conservation includes protecting animal habitats, preserving endangered species, and maintaining air and water quality. Every decision you make can contribute to accom- plishing these goals. For example, ensuring the safety of natural habi- tats provides animals with secure spaces to live and breed. Preserving biodiversity is crucial for maintaining the balance and resilience of ecosystems. Another vital aspect is guaranteeing the protection of endangered species. Many animals are at risk due to habitat loss, pollution, and climate shifts. By assisting with conservation initia- tives, you are supporting the creation of safe zones for these species to recover and thrive. Fresh air and clean water are necessary for people's and animals' well-being. It is essential to support initiatives   to prevent pollution in ecosystems to avoid the negative consequences it can bring to these resources.

You can still support conservation while having fun on your RV trips by participating in various ways. Giving to preservation groups is one of the simplest methods to have an impact. Organizations such as the World Wildlife Fund, The Nature Conservancy, and local park foundations utilize these resources to safeguard natural habitats, conduct research, and promote more robust environmental regulations.

Engaging in citizen science initiatives is also a great way to partici- pate. These projects frequently require gathering information on animals, flora, and environmental factors. The information from your observations can be valuable for scientists to understand and protect ecosystems. Backing environmentally conscious companies is another significant decision. By buying from businesses focused on sustainability, you use your purchase power to support a more ecologically friendly tomorrow. Search for companies that utilize eco-friendly materials, reduce waste, and support environmental initiatives.

Volunteering is a practical method to back conservation efforts. Plenty of parks and conservation groups provide volunteer opportunities ideal for RV travelers. Participating in park clean-up events is an excellent way to begin. These activities include collecting trash, upkeeping paths, and rejuvenating original plants. A choice is to engage in habitat restoration projects. These activities involve planting indigenous species, eliminating invasive plants, and revital- izing wetlands. Participating in wildlife monitoring programs allows you to help with significant research. These activities include moni- toring animal movements, documenting sightings, and assisting with tagging and relocation projects. These activities help the environment and create a stronger bond with the places you explore.

Engaging in sustainable tourism is essential for reducing your environmental footprint when traveling. Opting for sustainable travel choices can significantly lower your ecological impact. Choose routes that are fuel efficient, utilize public transportation when possible, and think about carpooling with other travelers. Abiding by sustainable travel principles helps prevent unintentional damage to the environment. This involves sticking to designated paths, considering animals, and reducing trash. Teaching others about sustainable tourism increases your influence. Spread the word by sharing your knowledge with loved ones and utilizing social media. The greater the awareness of sustainable travel practices, the more significant the impact.

Following these measures to promote conservation, you actively participate in a larger initiative to safeguard the Earth. The things you do, like giving to a conservation organization or participating in a habitat restoration initiative, have a tangible impact. By engaging in responsible tourism and backing eco-friendly enterprises, you contribute to developing a more sustainable global environment. This section has examined different methods to create a more environmentally friendly RV experience, including waste management and renewable energy sources. Afterward, we will explore safety and security to guarantee your travels are ecologically friendly and worry-free.

CHAPTER 6
SAFETY AND SECURITY

D uring the past summer, I encountered a difficult situation while exploring a secluded park in Idaho. I had chosen a picturesque path with poor signage, and unexpectedly, I ended up with a painful wound on my leg from a concealed tree limb. Luckily, my fully equipped first aid kit and basic skills came in handy. That situation emphasized the significance of preparing for unexpected RV camping events.

6.1 EMERGENCY PREPAREDNESS AND FIRST AID

Preparing a comprehensive first aid kit is the initial action in preparing for potential minor injuries or illnesses. Your package needs to have a variety of bandage sizes and gauze to protect cuts and scrapes. Antiseptic wipes and ointments play a vital role in cleansing wounds and averting infections. Remember to bring medications for pain relief and allergies. Using medical scissors and tweezers helps cut tape and extract splinters. Emergency blankets are essential for keeping warm during a sudden temperature decrease. Ultimately, a CPR mask can save a life by providing rescue breaths. Ensure you consistently inspect and refill your kit to ensure all items are current and prepared for use.

Creating a customized emergency plan for your camping excursion is also crucial. Begin by locating the closest medical centers and recording where they are situated. This information can be beneficial in a serious injury or sickness. Set up emergency contact information for loved ones who need to be informed in case of an emergency. Developing a communication strategy guarantees you keep in contact with your family and friends, even in areas with weak cell reception. Understanding the park's emergency procedures, such as evacuation paths and shelter spots, can assist in responding promptly and effectively during an emergency.

Acquiring fundamental first aid skills can greatly impact how emergencies are handled. Training and certification in CPR and AED can prepare you to manage cardiac emergencies efficiently. Properly managing cuts and burns can stop minor injuries from worsening. It is essential to handle allergic reactions carefully, particularly if you or someone in your group has documented allergies. Correct immobilization techniques for fractures and sprains can prevent additional harm and simplify transporting the injured individual to medical assistance. These abilities are beneficial for camping and important in daily situations.

It is crucial also to be ready for certain emergencies. Identifying signs such as feeling faint, queasy, and sweating excessively is crucial when addressing heat exhaustion and dehydration. It is important to relo- cate the individual to a cooler area, provide them with water, and use damp, cool cloths on their skin. Identifying and addressing hypothermia is essential in colder regions. Signs of the illness may consist of trembling, disorientation, and incoherent talk. The reaction includes gradually warming the individual with blankets, hot bever- ages, and body warmth. Dealing with insect bites and stings involves quickly decreasing swelling and avoiding allergic responses. Having an EpiPen for severe allergies could save your life. It is important to stay hydrated, rest, and consult a doctor if symptoms continue.

These preparations ensure you're ready for the unexpected, allowing you to focus on enjoying your RV adventure. Here's a checklist for your first aid kit to get you started:

First Aid Kit Checklist

- Various sizes of bandages
- Gauze pads or rolls
- Medical adhesive tape
- Antiseptic wipes and ointments
- Pain relievers (ibuprofen, acetaminophen)
- Antihistamines (Benadryl)
- Medical scissors and tweezers
- Emergency blankets
- CPR mask
- Sunscreen
- Anti-diarrhea medicine
- Ice packs and heat packs
- Eye drops
- Safety pins

- Sewing needle and thread
- Whistle
- Towel

Regularly restock and check the expiration dates of your first aid kit items to ensure everything is ready when needed. By being well-prepared, you can confidently handle minor injuries and emergencies, keeping your camping trip enjoyable and safe.

6.2 SOLO CAMPING: TIPS FOR SAFETY AND SOLITUDE

Camping alone can be fulfilling, giving you a special sense of independence and autonomy. Nevertheless, it also poses a series of difficulties and dangers. Sharing your travel plans with a trustworthy friend or family is important. Before departing, give them information about your camping trip, such as your itinerary, the parks you intend to visit, and when you plan to return. This ensures that people are aware of your whereabouts and anticipated return time. If your plans alter during your journey, be sure to adjust them. Regularly checking in can offer reassurance for both yourself and your family members.

Remaining in communication is another important element of ensuring safety while solo camping. In remote locations where cell service is not dependable, having a satellite phone or personal locator beacon can guarantee you have a means of seeking assistance in case of emergencies. These gadgets can transmit your GPS coordinates to emergency services without a cell signal. It is beneficial to consistently communicate through phone or messaging apps whenever service is available. Setting specific check-in times can guarantee that someone is aware of your safety. For example, establish a routine of checking in twice daily, in the morning and evening. This method enables faster dispatch of assistance in case of an emergency.

Choosing a safe campsite is crucial for solo campers. Opt for well-populated areas rather than secluded spots far from others. A campsite near park facilities like restrooms and ranger stations can offer an added layer of security. These areas are typically well-lit and monitored, making them less likely to attract trouble. Avoiding isolated locations can reduce the risk of encountering wildlife or unwelcome visitors. Always scout your campsite during daylight hours to ensure you're comfortable with the surroundings. Setting up camp before dark allows you to familiarize yourself with the area and spot any potential hazards.

Having the ability to defend oneself is crucial while camping solo. Enrolling in self-defense classes can provide you with skills to protect yourself in case of necessity. Several community centers and gyms provide these courses, which can help enhance your self-esteem. Having items such as pepper spray or a personal alarm can also give an extra feeling of safety. These objects are compact, portable, and very efficient in warding off dangers. Having a whistle or noise- making tool easily accessible is another uncomplicated yet successful tactic. A loud sound can surprise potential dangers and warn nearby campers about your situation.

Camping alone provides an opportunity for self-improvement and the pleasure of being by yourself, but it's essential to follow these safety measures. Sharing your schedule, keeping in touch, selecting secure camping spots, and learning self-defense techniques can help you experience the tranquility and independence of solo camping with reduced risks. These actions require minimal time but can significantly enhance your safety and help you fully appreciate the beauty and peace of your environment.

Camping solo provides a special opportunity to connect with nature and yourself deeply. Being alone can be very rejuvenating, enabling you to move at your own speed and appreciate your environment without interruptions. Nevertheless, it's important to balance this freedom and safety measures. The better you are prepared, the easier it will be to relax and have fun on your solo journey. Therefore, prepare your equipment, map out your trip, and follow these safety guidelines closely. Find peace in being alone, but remain vigilant and ensure your safety.

6.3   WILDLIFE SAFETY: COEXISTING WITH NATURE

It is important to know the wildlife in the area when camping in state parks. You may encounter several animals, each displaying unique behavior and potential dangers. Bears and mountain lions, while majestic, can pose a threat if agitated. Bears are naturally curious and might enter campsites looking for food. Mountain lions are harder to find but can be seen in places with thick forests and rugged terrain. Deer and elk are prevalent and typically docile, but it's advisable to maintain a safe distance as they may become hostile when they sense danger. Snakes and bugs are also commonly seen. Although the majority of snakes are not venomous, it is crucial to exercise caution and be able to recognize the venomous ones. Insects such as mosqui- toes and ticks can do more than just bother you; they can spread diseases.

Keeping your food stored securely is key to preventing unexpected interactions with wildlife. If you're in an area with bears, it's essential to have containers that bears cannot break into. These durable bins help protect your food and fragrant items, decreasing the chance of luring bears to your campsite. Storing food in your RV or car is also a beneficial habit. Ensure that all windows and doors are firmly shut. Immediately after eating, cleaning up food scraps and cooking areas is essential to prevent animals from being attracted. If provided, use an assigned dishwashing area, and always stay with your food. Always ensure your garbage is sealed correctly and kept at a distance from where you sleep.

Respecting the boundaries of wildlife is vital for both your safety and theirs. Watching animals from a distance prevents interference with their natural behavior or tempting them. Utilizing binoculars or tele- photo lenses for observation lets you examine things in detail while maintaining a safe distance. Refrain from interacting with or offering food to animals, even if it is tempting. Providing animals with food can lead to them depending on human food and becoming more inclined to come near campsites, posing risks for both the animals and campers. If you see wild animals, maintain a safe distance and silently savor the moment.

Having a good understanding of how to act in wildlife encounters can have a big impact. If you come across a bear, creating loud sounds can frequently scare it away. Speak loudly, applaud, or utilize a bear bell. If the bear doesn't go away, slowly move backward while watching it, but don't make direct eye contact. If you encounter a mountain lion, stand upright and maintain eye contact. Don't walk away or flee; elevate your arms and speak firmly and loudly to appear bigger. If you come across a snake, move away slowly. Most snakes will not pursue you and would rather be undisturbed. Using insect repellent can prevent mosquitoes, ticks, and other insect bites. Use it on both skin and clothes and again when necessary, particularly after swimming or sweating.

6.4 SECURING YOUR CAMPSITE AND RV

Ensuring the safety of your campsite and RV is crucial for a stress-free and enjoyable camping trip. Begin by fitting superior locks on both doors and windows. Numerous RVs are equipped with simple locks; however, improving to more secure choices can offer addi- tional peace of mind. It is recommended to consider wheel locks and hitch locks, particularly if you intend to leave your RV unattended for a period of time. Motion sensor lights can discourage possible intrud- ers. These lights turn on when motion is detected, lighting up your campsite and deterring potential intruders.

Another straightforward but successful tactic is to conceal valuable items from view. Keep valuable items like laptops, cameras, and other belongings in safe compartments or lockboxes. Make sure not to leave items outdoors overnight, even if you're in a seemingly secure loca- tion. Utilize curtains or blinds to obstruct the sight into your RV, increasing the difficulty for others to see what possessions are inside. Taking this small step can greatly decrease the chances of theft.

Developing relationships with nearby campers can improve safety and create a stronger sense of community. Spend some time presenting yourself and getting familiar with the people nearby. Creating a monitoring system to monitor each other's camping areas can be highly successful. Provide emergency contact details so they can notify each other quickly in case of concerns. This increases secu- rity and encourages a welcoming and helpful camping atmosphere.

It is extremely important to report suspicious activity. Inform park officials immediately if you see anything strange, like unfamiliar people near campsites or unusual sounds. Note any suspicious indi- viduals or activities and give as many details as possible. Contacting park rangers or security personnel can guarantee a prompt and professional resolution. Your attentiveness is essential for ensuring the safety of the entire park.

6.5   NAVIGATING REMOTE LOCATIONS SAFELY

When you venture into isolated regions, choosing your path is more than just selecting a destination. It's important to make sure you arrive and depart safely. Begin with trustworthy maps and GPS systems. Although paper maps may appear outdated, they are essential in technological malfunctions. Match them with a reliable GPS device or application such as Google Maps or Gaia GPS. Make sure to have offline maps downloaded when using these tools to navigate in areas without cell service. It is essential to check road conditions and weather forecasts before you depart. Being aware of potential weather changes helps you get ready for them efficiently. Additionally, locate places to refuel and take a break during the journey. GasBuddy and similar apps assist in finding nearby gas stations, preventing you from running out of fuel in remote areas.

Preparing your vehicle is just as important as planning your route. Start by carrying out a thorough inspection of the vehicle. Check your tire condition, brakes, and fluid levels. Ensure your lights are func- tioning correctly and your battery is in good condition. Having readily available spare tires and repair kits can help you avoid getting stranded. Having the right tools can turn a potential disaster into a minor inconvenience when dealing with a flat tire in a distant area. Ensuring your tank is full before beginning is logical, but it's also practical to have extra fuel available. Carrying a jerry can containing a few gallons of gasoline could be crucial for survival if you misjudge the distance to the nearest gas station.

Including emergency supplies in your preparation is vital and should not be ignored. Make sure always to have additional water and non-perishable food on hand. These items can help you stay nourished and hydrated in case you become stranded or delayed. Emergency shelter and blankets are crucial, especially when journeying through regions where the weather changes unexpectedly. A basic tent or emergency bivvy can offer shelter from the weather. Compasses and maps are crucial secondary tools for your GPS. Reading a map and using a compass can lead you back to safety if your electronic gadgets stop working. Having communication devices with backup power, such as a satellite phone or personal locator beacon, allows you to request assistance in emergencies. These devices can transmit your location to emergency services in crucial situations, potentially saving lives.

Remaining vigilant of your environment is essential when navigating isolated areas. Observing landmarks and trail markers lets you stay aware of your location, even if you stray from the main trail. It is essential to monitor time and daylight hours. Make sure you give yourself plenty of time to return to your campsite or vehicle before dark. Being caught in the wilderness after sunrise can be confusing and risky. Paying attention to the sounds of nature and environmental shifts can offer essential hints about your surroundings. The noise of flowing water can guide you to a stream or river, whereas the swishing of leaves can signal the presence of wildlife nearby. These natural cues can assist in keeping you oriented and alert to possible dangers. Knowing these specifics helps you do more than just navi- gate using a map; you can also genuinely grasp the surroundings and environment.

6.6   DEALING WITH EMERGENCIES AND UNEXPECTED SITUATIONS

Being adequately prepared for emergencies is extremely important during camping trips. It's more than just feeling calm; it's about acting promptly and efficiently in emergencies. Creating a plan lessens the effect of unforeseen circumstances, safeguards your well-being, and lessens the worry and tension associated with emergencies. Picture yourself far from the closest town when a problem arises—having a well-thought-out plan can be crucial. Being ready for any situation, whether a health problem, car trouble, or unexpected weather, helps you stay calm and handle it effectively, keeping yourself and your family protected.

Typical emergencies may involve medical problems, car issues, and severe weather or wildlife run-ins. Knowing how to administer first aid correctly can determine whether someone survives in critical situations. Knowing the correct method to clean and dress a wound is essential when dealing with a cut or burn. Keeping the injured area still is essential in a serious injury like a fracture or sprain until medical assistance can be obtained. Problems with cars malfunctioning are also common occurrences. Receiving aid from AAA or similar organizations can offer prompt help. Still, it is just as crucial to know about performing basic repairs like replacing a tire or jump-starting a battery. In natural disasters or extreme weather conditions such as unexpected thunderstorms or wildfires, it is important to remain adaptable and prepared to evacuate when needed. Handling wildlife encounters can be challenging; staying safe requires knowing how to react to animals like bears or snakes.

Your emergency kit needs to be thorough, encompassing various possible problems. First aid materials and medicines are essential. Include pain relievers, antihistamines, necessary prescription medications, and basics like bandages and antiseptic wipes. Tools and gear required for repairing vehicles are crucial. Consider items like a tire repair kit, jumper cables, and fundamental tools like wrenches and screwdrivers. Provisions for emergency food and water should consist of items that do not spoil and sufficient water to sustain for multiple days. Communication tools like radios and signal flares allow you to request assistance when your phone has no service. Having these items readily accessible can transform a potential disaster into a controllable one.

I can attest to the importance of developing and rehearsing an emergency plan. Having a plan written down is different from rehearsing it to ensure everyone is prepared for when it needs to be executed. Being aware of potential dangers and threats in your area can also provide advance notice of what to anticipate. Awareness of the indications and evacuation paths in wildfire-prone camping areas is crucial for survival. Establishing a web of emergency contacts is also a wise decision. These could be friends or family members who know your intentions and can help if things don't go as planned. Finally, remaining composed and concentrated in times of crisis is not as simple as it sounds, yet it is essential. Getting anxious only exacer- bates the situation; remaining composed enables clear thinking and efficient action.

CHAPTER 7
ENHANCING YOUR CAMPING EXPERIENCE

I recall a specific evening in Bryce Canyon National Park in Utah, lying on the roof of my RV, gazing at a sky filled with stars that looked within reach. The sky was adorned with the Milky Way, a stunning band of light, and I was amazed by the world's smallness and magnificence. The wonder of observing the stars lies in moments like these, which make you appreciate the enormity and grandeur of the cosmos. Whether you are experienced in astronomy or enjoy spending nights under the stars, state and county parks provide some of the top opportunities for stargazing.

7.1 BEST PARKS FOR STARGAZING

Certain parks are famous for lacking light pollution, creating optimal conditions for observing the stars. Utah's Bryce Canyon National Park is a destination that attracts stargazers with its exceptionally clear skies. The park also holds stargazing events and night sky programs with experienced rangers teaching about constellations and planets. Another fantastic spot to visit in Nevada is Great Basin National Park. Its isolated position produces minimal light pollution, classifying it as an International Dark Sky Park. One can observe countless stars during a clear night, as well as the Milky Way and a few planets, without the aid of a telescope.

Another hidden gem for stargazing is Big Bend National Park in Texas. The extensive landscapes and minimal human presence make it one of the top locations in the country for observing the stars. The park provides astronomy activities featuring telescopes avail- able for public use, offering a closer view of the wonders of the sky. Cherry Springs State Park in Pennsylvania, famous for stargazers, is located in the eastern direction. Renowned for its extremely dark skies, this location is one of the rare places in the eastern United States where you can fully appreciate the beauty of the Milky Way. The park features an astronomy area for observing the stars, including special concrete pads for telescopes and red lights to protect night vision.

A visit to Joshua Tree National Park in California is essential for indi- viduals residing on the West Coast. The park's great height and pure desert atmosphere are ideal for viewing the stars. Joshua Tree offers stargazing events like ranger-led night sky programs and astronomy workshops. Glacier National Park up north in Montana also provides a beautiful stargazing opportunity. The dark skies in the lower 48 states are due to the high elevation and remote location. In the summer, the park frequently offers ranger-led stargazing events.

Preparation is key for an optimal stargazing experience. Begin by verifying the lunar cycles and atmospheric conditions. During a new moon, stargazers can enjoy the brightest shine of stars due to the absence of moonlight. Monitor the weather forecast for clear skies, as they are also important. Stargazing applications such as Star Walk or SkyView can assist in recognizing celestial objects and organizing your evening. These applications utilize the GPS on your phone to display what can be seen in the sky from your current location, making it simple to locate constellations, planets, and satellites.

Locating the correct location is essential. Search for a spacious area far from artificial lights. Several parks have specific dark sky areas set aside to observe the stars. These locations have no light pollution, offering the optimal night sky view. Having the necessary equipment for stargazing can improve your enjoyment. Quality binoculars or a telescope can enhance the visibility of faraway stars, planets, and galaxies. Star charts and planispheres are valuable tools for recognizing constellations and monitoring the movements of celestial bodies. Having cozy seats and blankets is essential—lying on the ground can be uncomfortable and cold at night, even in the summer.

Several parks organize unique stargazing events and activities that enhance the overall experience. Night sky tours with guides, typically park rangers, offer interesting information about stars, planets, and constellations. These tours typically involve utilizing telescopes and other gear to provide a more detailed view of objects in the sky. Astronomy workshops offer a fantastic opportunity to learn about the night sky through hands-on activities. These workshops typically include telescope usage, astrophotography, and scientific explanations of celestial occurrences.

Meteor shower viewing parties are trendy. The Perseids in August and the Geminids in December attract many people to parks famous for their dark skies. These occasions frequently include informative presentations and interactive events, providing a wonderful opportunity to learn about the night sky while experiencing an amazing natural light display.

Observing the stars in state and county parks is a mystical encounter that deeply links you to the cosmos. Whether stargazing at Bryce Canyon, using a telescope at Great Basin, or joining a meteor shower event at Joshua Tree, these parks provide unmatched chances to discover the night sky. Grab your binoculars, pack a blanket, and visit one of these dark sky spots for a memorable stargazing experience.

7.2 PHOTOGRAPHY TIPS FOR CAPTURING NATURE

Capturing the beauty of nature through photography can be incred- ibly rewarding, and having the right equipment makes all the differ- ence. Investing in a DSLR camera is a good start if you're serious   about getting high-quality shots. These cameras offer superior image quality and flexibility compared to point-and-shoot models. Pair your DSLR with a variety of lenses to cover different scenarios. A wide- angle lens is perfect for capturing expansive landscapes, while a   macro lens lets you get detailed flora and fauna close-ups. Don't forget a telephoto lens for those distant wildlife shots. Next, a sturdy tripod stabilizes your camera, especially in low-light conditions or when using long exposure times. Look for one with easily adjustable legs and a reliable ball head. Filters, like polarizing filters, can enhance your photos by reducing glare and deepening the colors of the sky   and foliage. Keep a lens cleaning kit handy to ensure your lenses are always transparent and smudged-free.

When photographing landscapes and vistas, consider the time of day. Early morning and late afternoon, often called "golden hours," provide the best natural light. The soft, warm hues during these times can transform a scene from ordinary to magical. For stunning compositions, use the rule of thirds. Imagine your frame divided into nine equal segments by two vertical and two horizontal lines. Place key elements along these lines or at their intersections to create a balanced and engaging photo. Always look for leading lines, like a winding river or a path, to draw the viewer's eye into the scene. Capturing close-ups of flora and fauna requires a different approach. Patience is key. Wait for the right moment when the light hits just right, and focus on the details. For flowers, get down to their level to capture their beauty from a unique perspective. When photographing wildlife, a quiet and steady approach is essential. Use a fast shutter speed to freeze the action, and be ready to capture those fleeting moments.

Capturing wildlife in action can present difficulty but also lead to great satisfaction. Predict the animal's movement and utilize burst mode to capture several shots rapidly. This enhances your likelihood of experiencing that ideal moment. Take advantage of natural light. Cloudy days are suitable for taking pictures of animals because the soft light minimizes harsh shadows and bright spots. When shooting in bright sunlight, aim to place yourself so that the light is coming from the side to achieve a nice contrast and depth in your photos.

Improving and editing your photos can enhance the quality of each image. Tools such as Lightroom and Photoshop are effective software for this goal. Begin by modifying the exposure setting to ensure your photo is properly illuminated. Then, adjust the contrast to create dimension and emphasize your subject. Adjusting saturation and vibrance levels can boost the colors, giving them a vibrant look without appearing artificial. Another handy tool is cropping. It lets you eliminate distractions in the frame and concentrate on the primary subject. Consider how you want the viewer's gaze to move within the image when arranging your photo. A skillful photograph effortlessly leads the viewer from one focal point to another. Keep in mind that frequently, less is better. Occasionally, a straightforward piece with a definite topic can have a greater effect than a hectic, chaotic setting.

Sharing your photography with a broader audience increases the fulfillment you experience from your work. Constructing a digital portfolio or blog is an excellent method to display your top photographs. Platforms like WordPress or Squarespace provide simple templates for creating a professional website. Taking part in photography competitions can also serve as an effective way to enhance your skills and get noticed. Numerous parks and nature organizations hold competitions, allowing participants to showcase their work and potentially receive prizes. Social media platforms like Instagram and Facebook are ideal for posting your pictures to share with friends and followers. Utilize appropriate hashtags to expand your audience and engage with fellow nature photography lovers.

Photography is more than just preserving a moment; it entails showing your distinct view of the world. Proper equipment and tech- niques are important for capturing beautiful images of majestic mountain ranges, delicate flowers, or curious deer. Pack your camera equipment, venture into the outdoors, and unleash your creativity.

7.3 SOCIAL ACTIVITIES: MAKING FRIENDS ON THE ROAD

One of the most significant aspects of RV camping is the camaraderie that can be experienced while traveling. Participating in park activi- ties is an excellent way to socialize with other campers and build long-term relationships. Numerous parks host group hikes and nature walks, combining physical activity and social bonding. Picture yourself strolling through a woodland, receiving information about nearby plants and animals from a park ranger, and discussing with a fellow nature enthusiast. Campfire programs and storytelling sessions are commonly enjoyed. There is a special feeling to sitting by a fire, hearing stories of exploration, and possibly telling your own tale. These occasions frequently showcase regional legends and past events, blending entertainment with learning. Volunteer opportuni- ties and community projects offer another way for people to engage socially. Volunteering provides opportunities to contribute to the community and connect with people who share similar interests, whether through activities like cleaning up parks, planting trees, or participating in wildlife conservation projects.

Connecting with other campers can be as easy as saying hello to those camping next to you. A warm welcome and a grin can ease tension and create a positive connection. Involving RV clubs and virtual communities is also a great way to connect. Organizations such as Escapees RV Club and FMCA provide various resources and social interactions. You have the option to engage in forums, attend rallies, and take part in meetups. These meetings frequently include semi- nars, social activities, and team outings, offering many chances to establish new friendships. RV gatherings and gatherings are especially thrilling. They gather numerous RV fans for a brief period of enjoy- ment, education, and social interaction. From shared meals to fun activities, these gatherings offer a variety of ways to socialize with others. Attending some of these events can aid shy individuals in gradually gaining confidence in social situations.

Planning and coordinating your tasks can bring great satisfaction. Organizing a potluck meal at your campsite is an excellent way to unite individuals. Anyone can bring a dish to share, allowing you to socialize with your neighbors while sampling a range of food options. Organizing group gatherings and trips is another way to promote a feeling of togetherness within a community. Shared activities like hiking to a nearby waterfall, visiting a local museum, or kayaking on a lake can help form strong connections between people. Hosting game nights or movie nights can also be successful. Take with you a portable projector and a screen, arrange some chairs, and you have created an outdoor cinema. Engaging in board games, card games, or trivia nights can offer extended hours of amusement and fun.

Keeping in contact with the friends you meet while traveling has become simpler due to technological advancements. Trading contact details is a positive beginning. Contact information such as phone numbers, email addresses, or social media handles is crucial for main- taining connections. Platforms like Facebook and Instagram are excellent for keeping up with each other's travels and exchanging experiences. You can form a group chat or a private group to exchange photos updates, and make plans together. Another excellent way to sustain these friendships is by planning future trips together. If you get along well with another camper, consider meeting at another nearby park. Organizing your travel plans and destinations can result in shared experiences and fresh memories.

There are numerous ways to improve your camping experience through social interactions, whether you engage in park-organized events, connect with other campers, or plan your activities. The connections you make while traveling can enhance your experiences, establishing a community of fellow explorers with a mutual passion for nature. Do not hesitate - take initiative, participate, and enjoy the social aspects of RV camping.

7.4 BEST PARKS FOR RELAXATION AND TRANQUILITY

Discovering a serene and tranquil park can significantly enhance your camping trip. Certain parks are created to promote peace and calm, including designated quiet areas and restricted visitor numbers. Consider, for instance, the Boundary Waters Canoe Area Wilderness in Minnesota, which boasts over a million acres of untouched natural environment and over 1,000 lakes and streams; this destination is ideal for individuals searching for seclusion. The limited entry permits for the park guarantee that it remains uncrowded, offering a peaceful retreat for those wanting to get away from the busy routine of daily life. In the same way, Acadia National Park in Maine includes spots such as Isle au Haut, which can only be reached by boat and provides a serene and isolated escape.

Lakes, forests, and meadows are part of the natural landscape that enhances the peaceful atmosphere of a park. The tranquil setting for relaxation provided by Shenandoah National Park in Virginia includes rolling hills and dense forests. Skyline Drive in the park offers several parking spots to park your RV and enjoy the scenery. If you like being near a lake, think about visiting Caddo Lake State Park in Texas. The park's combination of cypress swamp and network of bayous results in a distinctive and relaxing ambiance ideal for relaxation. Often, these parks have rules for quiet hours and noise limitations to preserve the tranquil atmosphere, enabling visitors to enjoy the natural environment fully.

Engaging in relaxing and mindful activities can significantly improve your camping adventure. Engaging in yoga and meditation outdoors can be very centering. Picture laying your yoga mat on the gentle grass encircled by tall trees and the melody of birds chirping. Several parks, including Big Sur State Park in California, have specific areas for these activities, creating a perfect setting for practicing mindful- ness. Relaxing by the water while reading and journaling is another option. Discover a peaceful location near a body of water, arrange a cozy seat, and immerse yourself in a captivating book or your reflec- tions. Taking leisurely strolls in nature and observing birds can also be calming. Parks such as Everglades National Park in Florida provide boardwalk paths that lead visitors through tranquil surroundings, which are ideal for observing wildlife and experiencing tranquility.

Building a tranquil campsite requires some careful details. Begin by selecting a private and shaded location. Shade not only cools your campsite but also enhances privacy and seclusion. Arranging comfortable seating and hammocks can transform your campsite into a warm and inviting sanctuary. A strategically located hammock can provide an ideal space for a midday snooze or peaceful reading. Enhancing the ambiance can also be achieved by using soothing decor and lighting. Gentle, cozy lights hung around your campsite can produce an enchanting ambiance at night. Think about bringing some battery-powered fairy lights or lanterns to provide a soft glow in your area. A compact speaker emitting gentle music or natural sounds can enhance the soothing atmosphere.

Numerous parks provide wellness programs and amenities to enhance your relaxation experience. The popularity of nature therapy and guided mindfulness sessions is on the rise. These programs frequently include structured nature walks, meditation, and activities aimed at helping you form a deeper connection with the natural world and achieve inner serenity. Some parks, such as Hot Springs National Park in Arkansas, provide on-site massage and spa services. Picture yourself hiking and exploring during the day, then returning to your campsite for a soothing massage under the night sky. Some parks also offer wellness retreats and workshops. These occasions may vary from short yoga getaways to extended seminars on handling stress and overall well-being.

Places such as Red Rock State Park in Sedona, Arizona, are well- known for the wellness activities they provide. Renowned for its beautiful red rock formations and mystical vibes, Sedona draws in tourists from around the globe looking for rejuvenation and tranquil- ity. The park offers a range of health programs, such as guided hikes to vortex locations, where the earth's energy is believed to be particu- larly powerful. These encounters can be extremely revitalizing, making you feel centered and rejuvenated.

Engaging in activities like practicing yoga in nature, meditating beside a body of water, or taking a leisurely stroll can all help you discover serenity and calmness within the beauty of the outdoors. Creating a tranquil campsite and participating in wellness activities can enhance your experience, helping you relax and rejuvenate completely. There- fore, prepare your hammock, take a good book, and be prepared to explore some of the most tranquil and calm parks in the area.

7.5 APPS AND GADGETS TO IMPROVE YOUR TRIP

Improving your RV camping experience by utilizing suitable apps and gadgets can result in smoother, more enjoyable, and even slightly more thrilling adventures. Beginning with crucial camping applications that have the potential to improve different aspects of your journey greatly. Google Maps and AllTrails are essential for navigation and mapping purposes. Google Maps is excellent for overall navigation, assisting in locating directions, fuel stops, and nearby facilities. AllTrails, in contrast, is ideal for uncovering hiking paths, including user feedback, trail status, and difficulty rankings. Weather prediction applications such as Weather Underground are important in scheduling your plans and ensuring your safety. They offer thorough weather predictions, such as hourly updates and radar images, that can aid in avoiding unforeseen storms or extreme temperatures.

Field guide applications for identifying plants and wildlife have the potential to transform your camping adventure into a learning opportunity. Applications such as iNaturalist enable you to snap pictures of plants or animals and receive immediate identification assistance from a group of experts in the field of natural history. It's an amazing opportunity to discover native plants and animals, all while strengthening your bond with the natural world. Stargazing apps like Star Walk and SkyView are beneficial for enjoying magical nights under the stars. These applications utilize augmented reality to display the names and positions of stars, planets, and constellations when you aim your phone towards the sky. It enhances your stargazing experi- ence with an interactive element, increasing enjoyment.

Certain essential gadgets can significantly improve your RV camping experience. Portable solar chargers and power banks can be invalu- able, particularly when camping off the grid. They enable you to power your gadgets with solar power, ensuring you remain connected even in isolated locations. Bluetooth speakers can set a cozy vibe at your campsite by playing your favorite music or podcasts. A portable projector can transform any blank wall or DIY screen into your outdoor theater for movie nights beneath the stars. Thermostats and security cameras are also helpful smart home gadgets. A clever ther- mostat ensures a cozy temperature in your RV, while surveillance cameras offer peace of mind by monitoring your surroundings.

Remaining in communication while traveling is essential, particularly for digital nomads and individuals who rely on staying connected with loved ones. Utilizing Wi-Fi boosters and extenders can significantly enhance the quality of your internet connection. These gadgets boost weak Wi-Fi signals, helping users stay connected online even in areas with limited coverage. Selecting the appropriate mobile data plan is also important. Search for plans that provide sufficient data, excellent coverage, and the ability to include a mobile hotspot. Using your phone's data connection, you can access the internet on your laptop or other gadgets. Safely connecting to public Wi-Fi is also a significant factor to consider. It is important always to utilize a VPN (Virtual Private Network) to secure your internet connection and shield your data from cybercriminals.

Achieving a balance is key to enjoying technology while camping without detaining from the experience. Establishing restrictions on how much time you spend on screens can prevent you from constantly being attached to your devices throughout the day. Schedule dedicated time slots for checking emails, social media, and watching videos, and adhere to these set time limits. Finding a balance between using technology and engaging in outdoor activities is crucial. Utilize your gadgets to enrich your experience—such as utilizing a stargazing application to recognize constellations—but don't forget to set them aside and peacefully appreciate the beauty of the outdoors. Technology can serve as an excellent tool for education and discovery as well. Utilize educational applications to learn about the nearby ecosystem, geology, or history of the destination you are exploring. This doesn't just enhance your experience but also strengthens your admiration for the natural beauty surrounding you.

Adding these apps and gadgets to your RV camping arsenal can enhance enjoyment and reduce the stress of your trips. Having the proper technology can improve all aspects of your adventure, whether exploring new paths, forecasting the weather, keeping in touch, or staying entertained. Therefore, equip yourself with these items, and you will be ready for an amazing camping trip that combines modern technology with the timeless beauty of nature.

As we conclude this chapter, remember that using the correct equipment and some advance preparation can greatly improve your camping
trip. Next, let's move on to the following chapter, where we will
discover some secret advice and interesting finds to enhance your RV
travels.

CHAPTER 8
INSIDER TIPS AND HIDDEN GEMS

A couple of years ago, I discovered a hidden gem while wandering along the less-traveled roads of New Mexico. I arrived at the City of Rocks State Park entrance just as the sun set below the horizon. The scenery was otherworldly, with enormous volcanic rocks spread out like marbles on the desert ground. I didn't know this place existed, but it reminded me that the best adventures can be found off the usual route. This chapter focuses on lesser- known parks that, while not widely popular among tourists, provide memorable experiences.

8.1 LESSER-KNOWN PARKS WORTH EXPLORING

We will begin by visiting some parks that include unique geological formations. For example, the City of Rocks State Park is incredible with its tall volcanic rocks created more than 30 million years ago. These naturally formed monoliths form a maze of trails, ideal for both exploration and photography. Another sight to be noticed is Goblin Valley State Park, located in Utah. The park is renowned for its fanciful rock formations shaped like mushrooms, called hoodoos, that appear to come from a storybook. These one-of-a-kind geological formations offer a space for creativity and a setting for wonderful hiking experiences.

Next, think about parks that are often overlooked for their abundant wildlife. For instance, consider the Bosque del Apache National Wildlife Refuge in New Mexico. This secret oasis attracts bird enthu- siasts, especially during the yearly sandhill cranes and snow geese movement. Witnessing the sunrise and seeing thousands of birds flying is truly a magical experience. Another treasure is the Alligator River National Wildlife Refuge located in North Carolina. Although not as well-known as the Outer Banks, this area provides excellent chances to see black bears, red wolves, and different types of birds.

Sometimes, you only want to escape to a peaceful park surrounded by untouched natural splendor. One place like that is Blackwater Falls State Park in West Virginia. Famous for its breathtaking 57-foot waterfall cascading into a gorge surrounded by hemlock and red spruce trees, this park provides relaxing hikes and an opportunity to commune with the natural world. Caddo Lake State Park in Texas is also a peaceful location. Entering this realm with a maze of bayous and cypress trees covered in Spanish moss gives off the sensation of entering a different dimension. The serene journey through its rivers is ideal for anyone seeking relaxation.

The special characteristics of these parks are what set them apart. The rock formations at City of Rocks are not just for viewing from afar— you can camp right in the middle. Picture waking up encircled by old volcanic stones, with the Milky Way stretching above you in the evening. Goblin Valley provides a comparable charm, as its surreal scenery creates a beautiful setting for daytime discovery and night- time stargazing. The seasonal wetlands of Bosque del Apache foster a diverse ecosystem that sustains various wildlife, making each visit seem like a fresh adventure.

Accessibility can be problematic when visiting less popular parks, but with careful planning, these hidden treasures can easily be enjoyed. City of Rocks can be reached by a well-kept road from Highway 180, providing organized campsites and wilderness camping choices. Goblin Valley is conveniently located, with signs visible from Highway 24 and plenty of parking available. Both parks provide essential facilities such as bathrooms and designated areas for picnics, but it's advisable to bring your supplies due to limited nearby services.

Firsthand stories from other RV enthusiasts frequently offer the most valuable perspectives. One traveler described the eerie landscape of Goblin Valley as reminiscent of exploring Mars. They hiked among the hoodoos all day and took beautiful long-exposure photos of the stars at night. Another camper shared about their trip to Bosque del Apache, where they witnessed the breathtaking sunrise departure of countless birds, deeming it one of the most impactful natural displays they had seen.

A couple of hints can greatly help maximize these experiences. Make sure to bring durable hiking footwear and a camera for your trip to the City of Rocks to document all the different views of the one-of-a- kind terrain. Visiting Goblin Valley during the colder months is recommended to escape the extreme summer temperatures. A trip to Bosque del Apache is best during the busy migration season in

November, but there are still many chances to see wildlife even during slower times.

Uncovering these secret treasures brings extra thrill and satisfaction to your RV travels. Every lesser-known park provides a distinctive experience, whether the excitement of natural formations, the peace of pristine surroundings, or the delight of unexpected animal sightings. Therefore, veer off the beaten track and discover these enchanting locations. You never know what wonders are waiting right around the corner.

8.2 EXCLUSIVE DISCOUNTS AND MEMBERSHIP BENEFITS

Cutting costs can have a significant impact when traveling in your RV. Membership programs are helpful in that situation. To begin, we'll focus on the Good Sam Club. This program provides various advan- tages, such as savings at more than 2,400 Good Sam Parks throughout North America. You will also receive fuel discounts at specific gas stations and reduced RV supplies and accessories prices at Camping World and Gander RV & Outdoors stores. The club also offers road- side assistance and insurance choices designed for RV owners. Whether you're organizing a brief journey or a long-distance explo- ration, the Good Sam Club can assist you in cutting costs and jour- neying with tranquility.

Another wonderful membership scheme is Passport America. Famous for offering a 50% discount on campground fees at close to 1,600 campgrounds in the U.S., Canada, and Mexico, it is popular among travelers watching their budget. The savings can accumulate rapidly, particularly during a lengthy journey. Passport America members also get a guide that provides in-depth details on the campgrounds involved, assisting in effortlessly planning your stops. Some camping sites also offer bonus features such as complimentary Wi-Fi and use of recreational amenities. Many RVers rely on this membership due to the significant savings it offers.

Another great option is KOA Value Kard Rewards, especially for those who frequent KOA campgrounds. KOA sites provide a 10% discount on daily fees for their members during registration. The program   offers points for every visit that can be redeemed for perks like free nights and discounts on future visits. Families on road trips often choose KOA campgrounds for their family-friendly offerings, like swimming pools, playgrounds, and organized activities. In addition, the rewards program frequently offers exclusive deals, helping you make the most of your membership.

Check out the AAA RV Plus program as an AAA member. This bundle provides additional roadside assistance benefits specifically designed for RVs, including towing, tire replacements, and lockout assistance. AAA members are also eligible for discounts nationwide at various campgrounds, hotels, and attractions. The AAA campgrounds direc- tory offers crucial information on amenities, rates, and perks for members. With AAA RV Plus, rest assured, knowing that help is only a phone call away, regardless of your destination.

To maximize these membership benefits, consider combining discounts with off-season rates. Many campgrounds offer lower rates during spring and fall shoulder seasons, so planning your trips during these times can result in significant savings. Additionally, use your membership benefits for long-term stays. Some campgrounds offer reduced rates for extended stays, and combining these discounts with your membership perks can make your trip even more affordable. Participating in member events and activities is another great way to get the most out of your membership. Many programs host rallies, meetups, and special events where you can connect with fellow RVers, share tips, and make new friends.

Watch for limited-time discount codes and partner promotions with RV-related businesses. For example, Good Sam's Club often collabo- rates with companies to offer exclusive RV insurance, maintenance services, and camping gear deals. These promotions can provide addi- tional savings and enhance your RV experience. Some membership programs also offer special rates for book readers, so be sure to check if any exclusive deals are available.

Enrolling in these membership programs allows you to access various perks that enhance the affordability and enjoyment of RV camping. A membership program is tailored for you if you want to save on campsite fees, get into private campgrounds, or receive discounts on RV supplies and services. Therefore, register, use the discounts, and begin your journey with confidence that you are getting the most out of your money.

8.3 CONTRIBUTIONS FROM EXPERIENCED RV CAMPERS

Each RV enthusiast has their tale to share, and the combined knowledge of experienced nomads can provide valuable insights. Consider John and Lisa, who decided to sell their house and travel full-time. They discovered that managing work and travel was simpler than they had anticipated. John remembers when he parked their RV in a peaceful location in the Pacific Northwest and spent mornings working from there, then hiking through lush forests in the after- noons. They recommend purchasing a dependable internet system for those who live in an RV full-time. They utilize a mobile hotspot and signal booster to remain connected in remote locations.

Then there's Sarah, a solo traveler exploring the country in her compact RV for over a decade. Her journey began after retiring from a stressful corporate job. Sarah's approach to RV life is all about simplicity and self-sufficiency. She emphasizes the importance of regular maintenance to avoid costly repairs. Her top tips include keeping a detailed log of all maintenance activities and upcoming service needs. This habit has saved her from unexpected breakdowns more than once. Sarah also recommends joining local RV clubs and online forums to share experiences and gather tips from fellow solo travelers.

Families have their own unique set of experiences and challenges. With three kids and a dog, the Johnson family took a year off to travel across the U.S. in their RV. Keeping the kids entertained and engaged was crucial for a harmonious trip. They turned each destination into a learning opportunity, incorporating history, science, and nature lessons into daily activities. Their insider tip? Create a flexible schedule that allows for spontaneous adventures. This approach excites the kids and reduces the stress of sticking to a rigid itinerary.

For retirees and long-term travelers like Bob and Carol, the focus shifts to comfort and enjoying the journey at a leisurely pace. They've been on the road for seven years, savoring each stop. Bob swears to upgrade to a more comfortable mattress and invest in quality outdoor furniture. Carol adds that having a well-stocked kitchen with all the essentials makes a huge difference, especially when staying in less populated areas with limited dining options. Their favorite destina- tions include parks with rich wildlife and serene landscapes, such as Assateague Island, where wild horses roam freely.

Adventure seekers like Mike and Jess thrive on discovering new and challenging terrains. They've explored everything from Arizona's desert landscapes to Colorado's mountainous regions. Their unique experiences include off-roading adventures and backcountry camping, which they document on their popular blog. Their top advice is always to be prepared for the unexpected. They carry a comprehensive tool- kit, extra fuel, and a portable jump starter. For them, the joy of RVing lies in the freedom to explore off-the-beaten-path destinations.

Creating a sense of community is vital for many RVers. Connecting with contributors can provide further advice and camaraderie. Many seasoned travelers are open to sharing their knowledge and experi- ences through blogs, social media profiles, or RVing communities and forums. For instance, you can follow John and Lisa's travel updates on their Instagram page or join Sarah's Facebook group for solo RVers. The Johnson family has a YouTube channel where they share tips on traveling with kids, while Bob and Carol write a monthly newsletter filled with travel stories and practical advice.

Showcasing diverse experiences from various types of RV campers enriches the RVing community. Solo travelers and digital nomads offer insights on staying connected and safe on the road. Families with children provide tips on education and entertainment during long trips. Retirees and long-term travelers share their wisdom on maintaining comfort and making the most of each destination. Adventure seekers and outdoor enthusiasts inspire others to push their boundaries and explore new terrains. Each perspective adds value, creating a well-rounded resource for anyone looking to enhance their RV camping experience.

8.4   VIRTUAL TOURS AND INTERACTIVE CONTENT

Picture yourself inside your RV, enjoying a warm cup of coffee and discovering a beautiful state park without leaving your vehicle. The beauty of virtual tours is truly remarkable. Numerous state and county parks currently provide virtual tours on their official online platforms. These tours offer a wonderful chance to get a sneak peek of your upcoming destination or to relax in a new park without leaving home. Sites like the National Park Service (NPS) are excellent initial resources. They frequently showcase expansive views, thor- ough explanations, and occasional historical perspectives. As an example, you could virtually wander through Shenandoah National Park or delve into the detailed aspects of the Lyndon B. Johnson National Historical Park.

YouTube is also a valuable resource for exploring virtual parks. Many parks maintain YouTube channels where they upload videos of walk-throughs, drone footage, and tours led by rangers. These videos accurately understand the park's design, main attractions, and secret treasures. Platforms like "National Park Service" and "Parks Canada" contain many top-notch content. Moreover, VR applications such as Google Expeditions and Earth VR provide realistic experiences that simulate being in the actual location. Simply put on a VR headset, and you can discover the massive Redwoods or the wide expanse of the Grand Canyon.

Interactive maps are essential resources for organizing your RV trav- els. With Google Earth, you can zoom in on particular parks, see 3D terrain, and even access a street-level view of the park's roads and paths. Interactive park maps on various websites offer up-to-date details on trails, campgrounds, and facilities. These maps frequently use colors and symbols to represent different elements, helping you easily see your route and decide where to stop. Applications such as AllTrails provide up-to-date information on trails, including difficulty ratings, distance, elevation variations, and user feedback. Geocaching apps enhance hiking experiences by adding a fun treasure hunt element for adventurous individuals.

Multimedia content can enhance your camping experience to an even greater extent. Numerous parks offer park ranger video talks and webinars on their websites and social media platforms. These sessions discuss various subjects, including wildlife conservation and the park's history. Wildlife live cameras provide a real-time view of the park's residents, like the well-known bear cameras at Katmai National Park. These webcams offer an intriguing look into the everyday life of animals, helping you feel closer to nature. Online nature documen- taries and educational videos are excellent sources as well. YouTube and Vimeo contain numerous high-quality documentaries that explore the vegetation, animals, and geological aspects of state and county parks.

Participating in online communities and sharing your content can enhance your virtual experience—post links to virtual tours you have liked in RV forums and social media groups. Join online conversations about your preferred parks, trails, and camping advice. Numerous park websites and social media platforms invite visitors to share their photos and videos to showcase on the site. This assists in uncovering new locations for others and adds a personal element to the online experience. Participating in online park forums and discussion groups, such as those found on Reddit or Facebook, can offer valuable knowledge and promote a feeling of belonging within the RV enthusiast community.

Exploring new parks, planning future trips, and staying connected with nature are all made possible through virtual tours and interactive content, even when you're not traveling. These tools provide information and motivation, enabling you to maximize your RV excursions. Therefore, power up your laptop, take your VR headset and begin discovering the amazing virtual realm of state and county parks.

8.5 USER-GENERATED REVIEWS AND RATINGS OF TOP PARKS

Compiling user-generated reviews and ratings is like gathering stories around a campfire. Each one adds a layer of insight that can guide your next adventure. For instance, many RV travelers rave about the tranquility at Caddo Lake State Park in Texas. One reviewer mentioned the surreal experience of paddling through its maze of bayous under a canopy of cypress trees. Another highlighted the excellent bird-watching opportunities, noting sightings of wood ducks and herons. On the flip side, a few mentioned the need for better trail signage, which can confuse first-time visitors.

In contrast, some parks receive mixed reviews. Take Assateague Island, for example. While many love the wild horses that roam freely, providing a unique and enchanting experience, others caution about the mosquitoes and the need for effective bug spray. One family shared their joy of camping near the beach, waking up to the sound of waves, but also advised future visitors to pack extra stakes for their tents to handle the windy conditions. These detailed, honest reviews help paint a complete picture of what you can expect.

When looking at reviews, it's important to consider a range of experiences and perspectives. Families with children might focus on different aspects compared to solo campers. For instance, families might appreciate parks with playgrounds and organized activities, while solo campers might value solitude and quiet trails. Feedback on amenities like restrooms, showers, and Wi-Fi can vary widely, but seeing these different viewpoints helps you prioritize what matters most. One retiree shared their love for the spacious sites at Cape Disappointment State Park in Washington but noted that cell service could be spotty, which might concern digital nomads.

User-generated reviews are valuable because they provide real-world insights and experiences. They highlight potential issues and areas for improvement, offering tips and recommendations that you will only sometimes find in official park descriptions. For example, several Great Basin National Park reviewers mentioned bringing extra layers and blankets due to unexpectedly chilly nights, even in summer. Another traveler suggested checking local events in nearby towns, which can add a cultural twist to your camping trip.

If you want to contribute your reviews, being specific and detailed in your feedback is key. Mention both positives and negatives to give a balanced perspective. Including photos can help illustrate your points, whether the breathtaking view from your campsite or the less-than-ideal condition of a restroom. Personal anecdotes add depth and make your review more relatable. Sharing tips and recommendations, like the best time to visit a particular trail or a nearby diner with great coffee, can be incredibly helpful for future visitors.

By participating in this RV travelers community, you're assisting others and constructing a collective knowledge source that enhances everyone's adventures. Feedback can lead you to undiscovered treasures, alert you to possible dangers, and motivate you to visit new locations. Whether praising a stunning sunset or warning about a messy trail, your opinions have an impact.

8.6 FINAL TIPS FOR A MEMORABLE RV CAMPING EXPERIENCE

Remember that careful planning and preparation are crucial for your RV trips. Begin by charting your course, taking note of essential sights and places to take breaks during the journey. Make sure to keep your RV in excellent condition by scheduling regular maintenance inspec- tions. Prepare by purchasing necessary food, water, and first aid materials. A toolkit and spare parts can help you avoid unforeseen problems. Research your destinations in advance to find out what facilities and things to do are offered. A carefully organized vacation not only prevents last-minute anxiety but also enables you to maxi- mize your time spent outside.

The ability to locate the ideal campsite is crucial for the success of your trip. Utilize trustworthy applications such as Google Maps and AllTrails to assist you. Search for campsites that meet your require- ments, whether full hookups, pet-friendly locations, or close hiking trails. Arrive ahead to reserve the top places and allow yourself enough time to get comfortable before dark. After arriving, make sure to get to know the layout and facilities of the park. Knowing the loca- tions of the closest restrooms, trails, and emergency services can enhance your comfort and safety during your visit.

Maximizing the use of park facilities involves discovering the avail- able options. Numerous state and county parks provide various amenities such as laundry rooms, showers, and shared kitchens. These can enhance your experience, especially during extended stays. Utilize leisure amenities such as pools, play areas, and picnic spots. Join ranger-led activities and guided tours to learn about the park's past, animals, and environment. Engaging in these activities enhances your experience and allows you to connect with other campers to exchange stories.

Discovering unfamiliar locations and engaging in various experiences brings added thrill to your journeys. Feel free to explore parks that are not commonly known. Some of the most unforgettable moments can be discovered in less popular locations. Participate in outdoor activities such as kayaking, mountain biking, bird watching, or geocaching. Welcome the surprises and impromptu occasions, as they can often be the most memorable parts of your journey. Being willing to try out new experiences, like visiting a nearby festival or finding a secret path, can enhance the enjoyment of your trip.

Bonding with other campers and exchanging stories creates a feeling of belonging within the group. Become a member of RV clubs and engage with online communities to connect with fellow travelers who share similar interests. Participate in park activities and community service opportunities to contribute and meet new people. Building long-lasting connections can result from sharing stories, advice, and meals with fellow campers. Being part of the RV community can enhance your travels unexpectedly due to its camaraderie. Whether sitting by a bonfire or participating in an internet discussion, these relationships bring richness and happiness to your experience.

Continuing to learn and develop as an RV camper will maintain the excitement and freshness of your adventures. Participate in work- shops and training sessions on RV maintenance, outdoor cooking, and wildlife photography. Follow RV travel blogs and YouTube chan- nels for the newest advice, techniques, and locations. Exploring more books and guides about RV camping can offer fresh perspectives and motivation. The greater your knowledge, the more self-assured and daring you will be, enhancing each journey compared to the previous one.

As you complete your reading and prepare for your next journey, remember that the future is filled with opportunities. Every moment of your journey, whether carefully planned or unexpectedly diverted, contributes to your narrative. Accept the adventure, engage with people, and always keep discovering. The exciting adventure you've been waiting for is right on the horizon.

HELP OTHERS FIND HIDDEN GEMS —LEAVE A REVIEW FOR *STATE & COUNTY PARKS RV CAMPING* 🌲🚐

Hi there, adventure seeker!

Thank you so much for picking up *State & County Parks RV Camping: Discover Affordable, Hidden RV Gems in State & County Parks – The Ultimate Hassle-Free RV Road Trip Guide for Time-Saving Adventures!* We hope this guide has inspired unforgettable road trip ideas and provided helpful insights into finding those lesser-known, wallet-friendly camping spots.

If you enjoyed the book, I have a quick favor to ask that could make a big difference for future readers (and even for you down the road!). By leaving a review, you can help others looking for an affordable and meaningful camping experience in hidden state and county parks discover this book—and maybe even find their new favorite campsite.

So, here's the question: Would you like to help fellow RV adventurers find their own hidden camping gems?**

A quick review from you can guide someone who's just starting their own adventure and looking for advice. By sharing your experience, you're not just giving feedback; you're lighting the path for someone searching for that perfect RV getaway spot. Imagine helping someone else save time, avoid overcrowded places, or find the exact type of peaceful campsite you enjoyed.

Your honest review—whether it's sharing your favorite parts of the book, tips you found especially helpful, or feedback on what could be even better—will help other RVers decide if this guide is right for them. This simple act can go a long way and only takes a minute.

How to leave your review:

1. Head over to [Amazon](Amazon link here) or scan this barcode
2. Scroll down to the "Customer Reviews" section.
3. Click on "Write a Customer Review."
4. Share your thoughts! You don't have to write a novel—just a few sentences about what you liked or found useful is perfect.

The impact you'll make:

Leaving a review means someone just like you can make a more informed choice, skip the guesswork, and dive straight into the fun part of planning their trip. Plus, your feedback helps us keep improving our content to make each edition even more useful and enjoyable.

CONCLUSION

Wow, what an adventure we've been on together! As we wrap up this journey, let's take a moment to look back at the road we've traveled through this book. We've covered everything from planning RV trips to choosing the best state and county parks, understanding park facil- ities, engaging in exciting activities, and even focusing on eco-friendly camping.

Throughout the chapters, we've explored how to set your camping goals, whether you're seeking relaxation, adventure, or family bond- ing. Remember how we talked about tailoring your trip duration and activities to meet your needs? Those tips will ensure every trip is memorable for the right reasons. We also delved into the nitty-gritty of park amenities - from full hookups to pet-friendly sites and ample rig accommodations. By now, you should feel confident in picking the perfect park for your RV adventures.

Understanding park fees, reservation systems, and seasonal tips helped you navigate the financial and logistical aspects of RV camp- ing. We even shared some packing essentials and customizable itin- eraries to keep you well-prepared and flexible.

Navigating parks and finding the perfect campsites can be daunting, but with detailed maps, GPS coordinates, and insider tips, you can avoid getting lost and find those hidden gems. We also covered various amenities and comforts, such as laundry facilities, showers, and family-friendly areas, ensuring your stays are as comfortable as possible.

Activities are the heart of any camping trip. Whether hiking, fishing, bird watching, or scenic drives, we've highlighted some of the best parks and provided safety tips to keep your adventures fun and secure. And let's remember the importance of eco-friendly practices to preserve these beautiful spaces for future generations.

Safety and security are crucial, and we discussed everything from first aid preparedness to wildlife encounters and securing your campsite. These tips will help you handle any unexpected situations like a pro.

Lastly, we explored ways to enhance your camping experience with stargazing, photography, social activities, and connecting with fellow campers. We also introduced insider tips, hidden gems, exclusive discounts, and membership benefits to make your trips more afford- able and enjoyable.

Therefore, what are the main points to remember from everything discussed? Initially, having a plan is crucial. A clear idea of your travel goals and designing a well-thought-out itinerary will enhance the overall experience. Next, ensure you are always ready. Preparation is essential for a stress-free vacation, from having the correct equipment to knowing the park's layout. Thirdly, accept and welcome flexibility and spontaneity. Occasionally, the most memorable times come without any prior planning. Finally, show reverence for the environ- ment and engage in sustainable camping to maintain the beauty of these parks for all.

Here's a small request for you to take action. Use your newfound knowledge to begin organizing your upcoming RV expedition. Follow the guidance and recommendations provided in this book to ensure a memorable and extraordinary journey. Share your adventures with other RV enthusiasts, share your knowledge on online forums, and continue discovering new places. Don't forget to prioritize safety — always be ready for any scenario and follow the regulations of the parks you explore.

In my experience, RV camping has brought me much joy and contentment. Being awakened by birds chirping, the fragrance of pine trees, and the opportunity to explore unfamiliar places is genuinely magical. The connections I've made, the places I've been, and the peace I've found during my travels are priceless. This book will inspire you to start your adventures and find the same joy in RV camping that I have.

I appreciate you joining me on this journey. Whether you have some background in RV travel or are new to it, remember that the trip is brimming with countless possibilities. Stay inquisitive bold, and, most importantly, cherish each moment you encounter. Have a fun camping adventure, and I am excited to see you on our travels!

Safe travels and happy trails!

BONUS CHAPTER-OVER 300 LOCAL GEMS-OFTEN OVERLOOKED CITY, MUNICIPAL, AND COUNTY RV CAMPGROUNDS

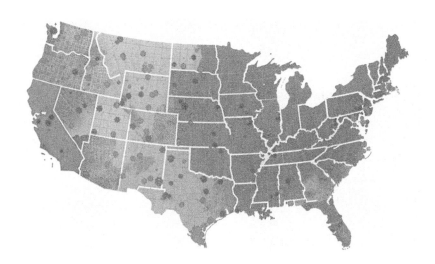

INTRODUCTION

This guide highlights a selection of municipal, county, and city parks in each state that RV campers often overlook. Compared to state parks, which are easily found on state websites, these local gems can take more work to discover. While not exhaustive, this list provides a solid overview of available options, giving you a valuable starting point for your next adventure. We hope you enjoy exploring these hidden camping treasures!

ALABAMA

County and Municipal RV Campgrounds in Alabama

1. Deerlick Creek Campground (Tuscaloosa County)

- **Location**: 12421 Deerlick Rd, Tuscaloosa, AL 35406
- **GPS Coordinates**: 33.3733° N, 87.5127° W
- **Website**: Deerlick Creek Campground
- **Amenities**:
  - Full Hookups: **Yes**
  - Electric: **50/30 AMP**
  - Water: **Yes**
  - Pets: **Yes**

2. Fairhope Municipal Pier Park (Baldwin County)

- **Location**: 1 Fairhope Ave, Fairhope, AL 36532
- **GPS Coordinates**: 30.5241° N, 87.9119° W
- **Website**: Fairhope Pier Park
- **Amenities**:
  - Full Hookups: **Yes**
  - Electric: **30/20 AMP**
  - Water: **Yes**
  - Pets: **Yes**

3. Foscue Creek Park (Demopolis, AL - operated by the U.S. Army Corps of Engineers)

- **Location**: 1800 Lock and Dam Rd, Demopolis, AL 36732
- **GPS Coordinates**: 32.5274° N, 87.8392° W
- **Website**: Foscue Creek Park
- **Amenities**:
  - Full Hookups: **Yes**
  - Electric: **50/30 AMP**

- Water: **Yes**
- Pets: **Yes**

4. Dauphin Island Campground (Mobile County)

- **Location**: 109 Bienville Blvd, Dauphin Island, AL 36528
- **GPS Coordinates**: 30.2519° N, 88.0853° W
- **Website**: Dauphin Island Campground
- **Amenities**:
  - Full Hookups: **No**
  - Electric: **50/30 AMP**
  - Water: **Yes**
  - Pets: **Yes**

ALASKA

County and Municipal RV Campgrounds in Alaska

1. Centennial Campground (Municipal - Anchorage, AK)

- **Location**: 8400 Starview Dr, Anchorage, AK 99504
- **GPS Coordinates**: 61.2246° N, 149.7469° W
- **Website**: Centennial Campground
- **Amenities**:
  - Full Hookups: **No**
  - Electric: **No**
  - Water: **Yes**
  - Pets: **Yes**

2. Chena River State Recreation Site (Municipal - Fairbanks, AK)

- **Location**: 3530 Geraghty Ave, Fairbanks, AK 99709
- **GPS Coordinates**: 64.8367° N, 147.7534° W
- **Website**: Chena River State Recreation Site
- **Amenities**:

- Full Hookups: **No**
- Electric: **No**
- Water: **Yes**
- Pets: **Yes**

3. Kenai Municipal Park (Kenai, AK)

- **Location**: 1400 Lowell Canyon Rd, Kenai, AK 99611
- **GPS Coordinates**: 60.5544° N, 151.2506° W
- **Website**: Kenai Municipal Park
- **Amenities**:
  - Full Hookups: **No**
  - Electric: **No**
  - Water: **Yes**
  - Pets: **Yes**

4. Homer Spit Campground (Municipal - Homer, AK)

- **Location**: 4535 Homer Spit Rd, Homer, AK 99603
- **GPS Coordinates**: 59.6282° N, 151.4971° W
- **Website**: Homer Spit Campground
- **Amenities**:
  - Full Hookups: **No**
  - Electric: **30 AMP**
  - Water: **Yes**
  - Pets: **Yes**

5. Seward Waterfront Park (Municipal - Seward, AK)

- **Location**: Ballaine Blvd, Seward, AK 99664
- **GPS Coordinates**: 60.1208° N, 149.4422° W
- **Website**: Seward Waterfront Park
- **Amenities**:
  - Full Hookups: **Yes**
  - Electric: **50/30 AMP**

- Water: **Yes**
  - Pets: **Yes**

6. Eagle River Campground (Municipal - Anchorage, AK)

- **Location**: 17729 Old Glenn Hwy, Eagle River, AK 99577
- **GPS Coordinates**: 61.3347° N, 149.5654° W
- **Website**: Eagle River Campground
- **Amenities**:
  - Full Hookups: **No**
  - Electric: **No**
  - Water: **Yes**
  - Pets: **Yes**

7. Skagway Municipal Campground (Skagway, AK)

- **Location**: Dyea Rd, Skagway, AK 99840
- **GPS Coordinates**: 59.4542° N, 135.3130° W
- **Website**: Skagway Campground
- **Amenities**:
  - Full Hookups: **No**
  - Electric: **No**
  - Water: **Yes**
  - Pets: **Yes**

8. Pioneer Park RV Parking (Municipal - Fairbanks, AK)

- **Location**: 2300 Airport Way, Fairbanks, AK 99701
- **GPS Coordinates**: 64.8391° N, 147.7392° W
- **Website**: Pioneer Park RV Parking
- **Amenities**:
  - Full Hookups: **No**
  - Electric: **No**
  - Water: **Yes**
  - Pets: **Yes**

9. Valdez Glacier Campground (Municipal - Valdez, AK)

- **Location**: Airport Rd, Valdez, AK 99686
- **GPS Coordinates**: 61.1344° N, 146.3756° W
- **Website**: Valdez Glacier Campground
- **Amenities**:
  - Full Hookups: **No**
  - Electric: **No**
  - Water: **Yes**
  - Pets: **Yes**

10. Portage Valley RV Campground (Municipal - Girdwood, AK)

- **Location**: 2435 Seward Hwy, Girdwood, AK 99587
- **GPS Coordinates**: 60.7895° N, 148.9555° W
- **Website**: Portage Valley RV Campground
- **Amenities**:
  - Full Hookups: **Yes**
  - Electric: **50/30 AMP**
  - Water: **Yes**
  - Pets: **Yes**

ARIZONA

County and Municipal RV Campgrounds in Arizona

1. Coconino County - Fort Tuthill County Park Campground (Flagstaff, AZ)

- **Location**: 2446 Fort Tuthill Loop, Flagstaff, AZ 86005
- **GPS Coordinates**: 35.1408° N, 111.6860° W
- **Website**: Fort Tuthill Campground
- **Amenities**:
  - Full Hookups: **Yes**
  - Electric: **30 AMP**

- Water: **Yes**
  - Pets: **Yes**

2. Maricopa County - Usery Mountain Regional Park (Mesa, AZ)

- **Location**: 3939 N Usery Pass Rd, Mesa, AZ 85207
- **GPS Coordinates**: 33.4656° N, 111.6164° W
- **Website**: Usery Mountain Regional Park
- **Amenities**:
  - Full Hookups: **Yes**
  - Electric: **50/30 AMP**
  - Water: **Yes**
  - Pets: **Yes**

3. Pima County - Gilbert Ray Campground (Tucson, AZ)

- **Location**: 8451 W McCain Loop, Tucson, AZ 85735
- **GPS Coordinates**: 32.2296° N, 111.1626° W
- **Website**: Gilbert Ray Campground
- **Amenities**:
  - Full Hookups: **No**
  - Electric: **30 AMP**
  - Water: **Yes**
  - Pets: **Yes**

4. Yavapai County - Watson Lake Park Campground (Prescott, AZ)

- **Location**: 3101 Watson Lake Rd, Prescott, AZ 86301
- **GPS Coordinates**: 34.5917° N, 112.4334° W
- **Website**: Watson Lake Park
- **Amenities**:
  - Full Hookups: **No**
  - Electric: **No**
  - Water: **Yes**
  - Pets: **Yes**

5. Maricopa County - Lake Pleasant Regional Park (Morristown, AZ)

- **Location**: 41835 N Castle Hot Springs Rd, Morristown, AZ 85342
- **GPS Coordinates**: 33.8549° N, 112.2761° W
- **Website**: Lake Pleasant Regional Park
- **Amenities**:
  - Full Hookups: **Yes**
  - Electric: **50/30 AMP**
  - Water: **Yes**
  - Pets: **Yes**

6. Pinal County - Picacho Peak State Park Campground (Picacho, AZ)

- **Location**: 15520 Picacho Peak Rd, Picacho, AZ 85141
- **GPS Coordinates**: 32.6350° N, 111.4005° W
- **Website**: Picacho Peak State Park
- **Amenities**:
  - Full Hookups: **Yes**
  - Electric: **50/30 AMP**
  - Water: **Yes**
  - Pets: **Yes**

7. Coconino County - Kaibab Lake Campground (Williams, AZ)

- **Location**: 11 miles NW of Williams, AZ 86046
- **GPS Coordinates**: 35.3149° N, 112.1660° W
- **Website**: Kaibab Lake Campground
- **Amenities**:
  - Full Hookups: **No**
  - Electric: **No**
  - Water: **Yes**
  - Pets: **Yes**

8. Pinal County - McFarland State Historic Park (Florence, AZ)

- **Location**: 24 W Ruggles St, Florence, AZ 85132
- **GPS Coordinates**: 33.0312° N, 111.3871° W
- **Website**: McFarland State Historic Park
- **Amenities**:
  - Full Hookups: **No**
  - Electric: **No**
  - Water: **No**
  - Pets: **Yes**

9. Yuma County - West Wetlands RV Park (Yuma, AZ)

- **Location**: 282 N 12th Ave, Yuma, AZ 85364
- **GPS Coordinates**: 32.7267° N, 114.6317° W
- **Website**: West Wetlands Park
- **Amenities**:
  - Full Hookups: **Yes**
  - Electric: **50/30 AMP**
  - Water: **Yes**
  - Pets: **Yes**

10. Maricopa County - White Tank Mountain Regional Park (Waddell, AZ)

- **Location**: 20304 W White Tank Mountain Rd, Waddell, AZ 85355
- **GPS Coordinates**: 33.5734° N, 112.5834° W
- **Website**: White Tank Mountain Regional Park
- **Amenities**:
  - Full Hookups: **Yes**
  - Electric: **50/30 AMP**
  - Water: **Yes**
  - Pets: **Yes**

11. Mohave County - Davis Camp Park (Bullhead City, AZ)

- **Location**: 2251 Hwy 68, Bullhead City, AZ 86429
- **GPS Coordinates**: 35.1845° N, 114.5730° W
- **Website**: Davis Camp Park
- **Amenities**:
  - Full Hookups: **Yes**
  - Electric: **50/30 AMP**
  - Water: **Yes**
  - Pets: **Yes**

12. Coconino County - Pine Flat Campground (Sedona, AZ)

- **Location**: 6701 AZ-89A, Sedona, AZ 86336
- **GPS Coordinates**: 34.9483° N, 111.7546° W
- **Website**: Pine Flat Campground
- **Amenities**:
  - Full Hookups: **No**
  - Electric: **No**
  - Water: **Yes**
  - Pets: **Yes**

ARKANSAS

County and Municipal RV Campgrounds in Arkansas

1. Craighead Forest Park (Jonesboro, AR - Municipal)

- **Location**: 4910 S Culberhouse Rd, Jonesboro, AR 72404
- **GPS Coordinates**: 35.7907° N, 90.7156° W
- **Website**: Craighead Forest Park
- **Amenities**:
  - Full Hookups: **Yes**
  - Electric: **50/30 AMP**
  - Water: **Yes**

- Pets: **Yes**

2. Dam Site Park (Heber Springs, AR - Cleburne County)

- **Location**: 700 Heber Springs Rd N, Heber Springs, AR 72543
- **GPS Coordinates**: 35.4910° N, 92.0464° W
- **Website**: Dam Site Park
- **Amenities**:
  - Full Hookups: **No**
  - Electric: **30 AMP**
  - Water: **Yes**
  - Pets: **Yes**

3. Maumelle Park (Little Rock, AR - Municipal)

- **Location**: 9009 Pinnacle Valley Rd, Little Rock, AR 72223
- **GPS Coordinates**: 34.8121° N, 92.4444° W
- **Website**: Maumelle Park
- **Amenities**:
  - Full Hookups: **Yes**
  - Electric: **50/30 AMP**
  - Water: **Yes**
  - Pets: **Yes**

4. Burns Park RV Park (North Little Rock, AR - Municipal)

- **Location**: 4101 Arlene Layman Dr, North Little Rock, AR 72118
- **GPS Coordinates**: 34.7969° N, 92.3641° W
- **Website**: Burns Park RV Park
- **Amenities**:
  - Full Hookups: **Yes**
  - Electric: **50/30 AMP**
  - Water: **Yes**
  - Pets: **Yes**

5. Prairie Creek Campground (Rogers, AR - Benton County)

- **Location**: 9300 N Park Rd, Rogers, AR 72756
- **GPS Coordinates**: 36.3351° N, 94.0387° W
- **Website**: Prairie Creek Campground
- **Amenities**:
  - Full Hookups: **No**
  - Electric: **50/30 AMP**
  - Water: **Yes**
  - Pets: **Yes**

6. Shady Lake Recreation Area (Umpire, AR - Howard County)

- **Location**: 85 Shady Lake Rd, Umpire, AR 71971
- **GPS Coordinates**: 34.3767° N, 93.9679° W
- **Website**: Shady Lake Recreation Area
- **Amenities**:
  - Full Hookups: **No**
  - Electric: **No**
  - Water: **Yes**
  - Pets: **Yes**

7. Springhill Park (Barling, AR - Sebastian County)

- **Location**: 1700 Lock and Dam Rd, Barling, AR 72923
- **GPS Coordinates**: 35.2922° N, 94.3084° W
- **Website**: Springhill Park
- **Amenities**:
  - Full Hookups: **Yes**
  - Electric: **50/30 AMP**
  - Water: **Yes**
  - Pets: **Yes**

8. Beaverfork Lake Park (Conway, AR - Municipal)

- **Location**: 20 Kinley Dr, Conway, AR 72032
- **GPS Coordinates**: 35.1252° N, 92.4949° W
- **Website**: Beaverfork Lake Park
- **Amenities**:
  - Full Hookups: **No**
  - Electric: **No**
  - Water: **No**
  - Pets: **Yes**

CALIFORNIA

County and Municipal RV Campgrounds in California

1. Santa Clara County - Coyote Lake Harvey Bear Ranch (Gilroy, CA)

- **Location: 10840 Coyote Lake Rd, Gilroy, CA 95020**
- **GPS Coordinates: 37.0874° N, 121.5185° W**
- **Website: Coyote Lake Harvey Bear Ranch**
- **Amenities:**
  - **Full Hookups: Yes**
  - **Electric: 30 AMP**
  - **Water: Yes**
  - **Pets: Yes**

2. Monterey County - Laguna Seca Recreation Area (Salinas, CA)

- **Location: 1025 Monterey Salinas Hwy, Salinas, CA 93908**
- **GPS Coordinates: 36.5827° N, 121.7547° W**
- **Website: Laguna Seca Recreation Area**
- **Amenities:**
  - Full Hookups: Yes
  - **Electric: 50/30 AMP**

- ○ Water: Yes
- ○ Pets: Yes

3. San Diego County - Agua Caliente County Park (Julian, CA)

- Location: 39555 Great Southern Overland Stage Route, Julian, CA 92036
- GPS Coordinates: 32.9575° N, 116.3058° W
- Website: Agua Caliente County Park
- Amenities:
  - ○ Full Hookups: Yes
  - ○ Electric: 50/30 AMP
  - ○ Water: Yes
  - ○ Pets: Yes

4. Orange County - O'Neill Regional Park (Trabuco Canyon, CA)

- Location: 30892 Trabuco Canyon Rd, Trabuco Canyon, CA 92679
- GPS Coordinates: 33.6834° N, 117.5880° W
- Website: O'Neill Regional Park
- Amenities:
  - ○ Full Hookups: No
  - ○ Electric: 30 AMP
  - ○ Water: Yes
  - ○ Pets: Yes

5. Buena Vista Aquatic Recreation Area (Kern County - Bakersfield)

- Location: 13601 Ironbark Rd, Bakersfield, CA 93311
- GPS Coordinates: 35.2557° N, 119.3190° W
- Website: Buena Vista Aquatic Recreation Area
- Amenities:
  - ○ Full Hookups: Yes

- Electric: 50/30 AMP
- Water: Yes
- Pets: Yes

6. Lake Cahuilla Veterans Regional Park (Riverside County)

- Location: 58075 Jefferson St, La Quinta, CA 92253
- GPS Coordinates: 33.6186° N, 116.2615° W
- Website: Lake Cahuilla Veterans Regional Park
- Amenities:
  - Full Hookups: Yes
  - Electric: 50/30 AMP
  - Water: Yes
  - Pets: Yes

7. Cachuma Lake Recreation Area (Santa Barbara County)

- Location: 2225 CA-154, Santa Barbara, CA 93105
- GPS Coordinates: 34.5859° N, 119.9671° W
- Website: Cachuma Lake Recreation Area
- Amenities:
  - Full Hookups: Yes
  - Electric: 50/30 AMP
  - Water: Yes
  - Pets: Yes

8. Castaic Lake Recreation Area (Los Angeles County)

- Location: 32132 Castaic Lake Dr, Castaic, CA 91384
- GPS Coordinates: 34.5073° N, 118.6103° W
- Website: Castaic Lake Recreation Area
- Amenities:
  - Full Hookups: Yes
  - Electric: 50/30 AMP
  - Water: Yes

◦ Pets: Yes

9. O'Neill Regional Park (Orange County)

- Location: 30892 Trabuco Canyon Rd, Trabuco Canyon, CA 92678
- GPS Coordinates: 33.6783° N, 117.5716° W
- Website: O'Neill Regional Park
- Amenities:
  - ◦ Full Hookups: Yes
  - ◦ Electric: 50/30 AMP
  - ◦ Water: Yes
  - ◦ Pets: Yes

10. San Mateo County - Coyote Point Recreation Area

- Location: 1701 Coyote Point Dr, San Mateo, CA 94401
- GPS Coordinates: 37.5869° N, 122.3192° W
- Website: San Mateo County Parks
- Amenities:
  - ◦ Full Hookups: No
  - ◦ Electric: 30 AMP
  - ◦ Water: Yes
  - ◦ Pets: Yes (leash required)

11. San Diego County - Guajome Regional Park

- Location: 3000 Guajome Lake Rd, Oceanside, CA 92057
- GPS Coordinates: 33.2434° N, 117.2825° W
- Website: San Diego County Parks
- Amenities:
  - ◦ Full Hookups: Yes
  - ◦ Electric: 30/50 AMP
  - ◦ Water: Yes
  - ◦ Pets: Yes

12. Alameda County - Del Valle Regional Park

- Location: 7000 Del Valle Rd, Livermore, CA 94550
- GPS Coordinates: 37.5700° N, 121.7080° W
- Website: East Bay Regional Parks
- Amenities:
  - Full Hookups: No
  - Electric: 30 AMP
  - Water: Yes
  - Pets: Yes (with restrictions)

13. Sacramento County - Gibson Ranch Regional Park

- Location: 8556 Gibson Ranch Park Rd, Elverta, CA 95626
- GPS Coordinates: 38.7071° N, 121.4088° W
- Website: Gibson Ranch
- Amenities:
  - Full Hookups: Yes
  - Electric: 30 AMP
  - Water: Yes
  - Pets: Yes

14. Yucaipa Regional Park

- Location: 33900 Oak Glen Rd, Yucaipa, CA 92399
- GPS Coordinates: 34.0418° N, 117.0406° W
- Website: San Bernardino County Regional Parks
- Amenities:
  - Full Hookups: Yes
  - Electric: 30/50 AMP
  - Water: Yes
  - Pets: Yes (leash required)

15. Prado Regional Park

- Location: 16700 Euclid Ave, Chino, CA 91708
- GPS Coordinates: 33.9512° N, 117.6384° W
- Website: Prado Regional Park
- Amenities:
  - Full Hookups: Yes
  - Electric: 30/50 AMP
  - Water: Yes
  - Pets: Yes (leash required)

16. Mojave Narrows Regional Park

- Location: 18000 Yates Rd, Victorville, CA 92392
- GPS Coordinates: 34.5395° N, 117.2903° W
- Website: Mojave Narrows Regional Park
- Amenities:
  - Full Hookups: Yes
  - Electric: 30 AMP
  - Water: Yes
  - Pets: Yes (leash required)

COLORADO

County and Municipal RV Campgrounds in Colorado

1. Boulder County - Boulder County Fairgrounds Campground (Longmont, CO)

- Location: 9595 Nelson Rd, Longmont, CO 80501
- GPS Coordinates: 40.1636° N, 105.1171° W
- Website: Boulder County Fairgrounds Campground
- Amenities:
  - Full Hookups: Yes
  - Electric: 50/30 AMP

- Water: **Yes**
- Pets: **Yes**

2. Jefferson County - Bear Creek Lake Park Campground (Lakewood, CO)

- **Location**: 15600 W Morrison Rd, Lakewood, CO 80228
- **GPS Coordinates**: 39.6506° N, 105.1518° W
- **Website**: Bear Creek Lake Park
- **Amenities**:
  - Full Hookups: **Yes**
  - Electric: **50/30 AMP**
  - Water: **Yes**
  - Pets: **Yes**

3. Chaffee County - Salida East Campground (Salida, CO)

- **Location**: Salida East River Park Rd, Salida, CO 81201
- **GPS Coordinates**: 38.5156° N, 106.0048° W
- **Website**: Salida East Campground
- **Amenities**:
  - Full Hookups: **No**
  - Electric: **No**
  - Water: **Yes**
  - Pets: **Yes**

4. Gunnison County - Blue Mesa Reservoir (Elk Creek Campground)

- **Location**: 102 Elk Creek, Gunnison, CO 81230
- **GPS Coordinates**: 38.4632° N, 107.0343° W
- **Website**: Elk Creek Campground
- **Amenities**:
  - Full Hookups: **No**
  - Electric: **50/30 AMP**

- ◦ Water: **Yes**
- ◦ Pets: **Yes**

5. Larimer County - Carter Lake Reservoir Campground (Loveland, CO)

- **Location**: 1800 S County Rd 31, Loveland, CO 80537
- **GPS Coordinates**: 40.3392° N, 105.1973° W
- **Website**: Carter Lake Campground
- **Amenities**:
  - ◦ Full Hookups: **Yes**
  - ◦ Electric: **50/30 AMP**
  - ◦ Water: **Yes**
  - ◦ Pets: **Yes**

CONNECTICUT

County and Municipal RV Campgrounds in Connecticut

None

DELAWARE

County and Municipal RV Campgrounds in Delaware

1. Prime Hook National Wildlife Refuge Campground (Sussex County, DE)

- **Location**: 11978 Turkle Pond Rd, Milton, DE 19968
- **GPS Coordinates**: 38.8356° N, 75.2277° W
- **Website**: Prime Hook National Wildlife Refuge
- **Amenities**:
  - ◦ Full Hookups: **No**
  - ◦ Electric: **No**
  - ◦ Water: **No**
  - ◦ Pets: **Yes (in designated areas)**

FLORIDA

County and Municipal RV Campgrounds in Florida

1. Long Point Park Campground (Brevard County)

- **Location**: 700 Long Point Rd, Melbourne Beach, FL 32951
- **GPS Coordinates**: 27.8769° N, 80.4927° W
- **Website**: Long Point Park
- **Amenities**:
  - Full Hookups: **Yes**
  - Electric: **50/30 AMP**
  - Water: **Yes**
  - Pets: **Yes**

2. Fort De Soto Park Campground (Pinellas County)

- **Location**: 3500 Pinellas Bayway S, Tierra Verde, FL 33715
- **GPS Coordinates**: 27.6274° N, 82.7349° W
- **Website**: Fort De Soto Park
- **Amenities**:
  - Full Hookups: **Yes**
  - Electric: **50/30 AMP**
  - Water: **Yes**
  - Pets: **Yes (in designated areas)**

3. John Prince Park Campground (Palm Beach County)

- **Location**: 4759 S Congress Ave, Lake Worth, FL 33461
- **GPS Coordinates**: 26.5982° N, 80.0880° W
- **Website**: John Prince Park
- **Amenities**:
  - Full Hookups: **Yes**
  - Electric: **50/30 AMP**
  - Water: **Yes**

○ Pets: **Yes**

4. Larry and Penny Thompson Memorial Park Campground (Miami-Dade County)

- **Location**: 12451 SW 184th St, Miami, FL 33177
- **GPS Coordinates**: 25.5951° N, 80.3965° W
- **Website**: Larry and Penny Thompson Park
- **Amenities**:
  ○ Full Hookups: **Yes**
  ○ Electric: **50/30 AMP**
  ○ Water: **Yes**
  ○ Pets: **Yes**

GEORGIA

County and Municipal RV Campgrounds in Georgia

1. River Forks Park and Campground (Hall County)

- **Location**: 3500 Keith Bridge Rd, Gainesville, GA 30504
- **GPS Coordinates**: 34.3133° N, 83.9144° W
- **Website**: River Forks Park
- **Amenities**:
  ○ Full Hookups: **Yes**
  ○ Electric: **50/30 AMP**
  ○ Water: **Yes**
  ○ Pets: **Yes**

2. Blythe Island Regional Park Campground (Glynn County)

- **Location**: 6616 Blythe Island Hwy, Brunswick, GA 31523
- **GPS Coordinates**: 31.1761° N, 81.5239° W
- **Website**: Blythe Island Regional Park
- **Amenities**:

- Full Hookups: **Yes**
  - Electric: **50/30 AMP**
  - Water: **Yes**
  - Pets: **Yes**

3. McIntosh Reserve Park Campground (Carroll County)

- **Location**: 1046 W McIntosh Cir, Whitesburg, GA 30185
- **GPS Coordinates**: 33.4511° N, 84.9487° W
- **Website**: McIntosh Reserve Park
- **Amenities**:
  - Full Hookups: **No**
  - Electric: **30 AMP**
  - Water: **Yes**
  - Pets: **Yes**

HAWAII

Hawaii has limited options for traditional RV camping due to its unique geographical location and environmental regulations. The islands have a different RV infrastructure than found on the mainland United States, and most county and municipal parks focus on tent camping or cabin rentals. Additionally, rental or privately owned RVs are rare in Hawaii, and strict laws about overnight vehicle stays restrict where RVs can park.

IDAHO

County and Municipal RV Campgrounds in Idaho

1. North Fork Campground (Clark County)

- **Location**: 449 E Anderson St, Dubois, ID 83423
- **GPS Coordinates**: 44.1740° N, 112.2333° W
- **Website**: North Fork Campground

- **Amenities**:
  - Full Hookups: **No**
  - Electric: **No**
  - Water: **Yes**
  - Pets: **Yes**

ILLINOIS

County and Municipal RV Campgrounds in Illinois

1. Paul Wolff Campground (Kane County)

- **Location**: 38W235 Big Timber Rd, Elgin, IL 60124
- **GPS Coordinates**: 42.0542° N, 88.3808° W
- **Website**: Paul Wolff Campground
- **Amenities**:
  - Full Hookups: **Yes**
  - Electric: **50/30 AMP**
  - Water: **Yes**
  - Pets: **Yes**

2. Camp Sullivan (Cook County)

- **Location**: 14630 Oak Park Ave, Oak Forest, IL 60452
- **GPS Coordinates**: 41.6255° N, 87.7742° W
- **Website**: Camp Sullivan
- **Amenities**:
  - Full Hookups: **No**
  - Electric: **30 AMP**
  - Water: **Yes**
  - Pets: **Yes**

3. Shabbona Lake State Recreation Area (DeKalb County)

- **Location**: 4201 Shabbona Grove Rd, Shabbona, IL 60550
- **GPS Coordinates**: 41.7514° N, 88.8709° W
- **Website**: Shabbona Lake State Park
- **Amenities**:
  - Full Hookups: **No**
  - Electric: **30/20 AMP**
  - Water: **Yes**
  - Pets: **Yes**

4. Illiniwek Forest Preserve Campground (Rock Island County)

- **Location**: 836 State Ave, Hampton, IL 61256
- **GPS Coordinates**: 41.5641° N, 90.4071° W
- **Website**: Illiniwek Forest Preserve
- **Amenities**:
  - Full Hookups: **Yes**
  - Electric: **50/30 AMP**
  - Water: **Yes**
  - Pets: **Yes**

INDIANA

County and Municipal RV Campgrounds in Indiana

1. White River Campground (Hamilton County)

- **Location**: 11299 E 234th St, Cicero, IN 46034
- **GPS Coordinates**: 40.1293° N, 86.0116° W
- **Website**: White River Campground
- **Amenities**:
  - Full Hookups: **Yes**
  - Electric: **50/30 AMP**
  - Water: **Yes**

○ Pets: **Yes**

2. Lake Monroe Village (Monroe County)

- **Location**: 8107 S Fairfax Rd, Bloomington, IN 47401
- **GPS Coordinates**: 39.0364° N, 86.4997° W
- **Website**: <u>Lake Monroe Village</u>
- **Amenities**:
  - ○ Full Hookups: **Yes**
  - ○ Electric: **50/30 AMP**
  - ○ Water: **Yes**
  - ○ Pets: **Yes**

3. Brookville Lake Campgrounds (Franklin County)

- **Location**: 14108 State Road 101, Brookville, IN 47012
- **GPS Coordinates**: 39.4697° N, 84.9996° W
- **Website**: Brookville Lake
- **Amenities**:
  - ○ Full Hookups: **No**
  - ○ Electric: **50/30 AMP**
  - ○ Water: **Yes**
  - ○ Pets: **Yes**

IOWA

County and Municipal RV Campgrounds in Iowa

1. Squaw Creek Park (Linn County)

- **Location**: 4305 Squaw Ln, Marion, IA 52302
- **GPS Coordinates**: 42.0282° N, 91.5859° W
- **Website**: Squaw Creek Park
- **Amenities**:
  - ○ Full Hookups: **Yes**

- Electric: **50/30 AMP**
- Water: **Yes**
- Pets: **Yes**

2. Big Woods Lake Campground (Black Hawk County)

- **Location**: 1501 E Big Woods Rd, Cedar Falls, IA 50613
- **GPS Coordinates**: 42.5442° N, 92.4686° W
- **Website**: Big Woods Lake Campground
- **Amenities**:
  - Full Hookups: **Yes**
  - Electric: **50/30 AMP**
  - Water: **Yes**
  - Pets: **Yes**

3. Cherry Glen Campground (Polk County)

- **Location**: 5600 NW 78th Ave, Johnston, IA 50131
- **GPS Coordinates**: 41.7399° N, 93.7007° W
- **Website**: Cherry Glen Campground
- **Amenities**:
  - Full Hookups: **No**
  - Electric: **50/30 AMP**
  - Water: **Yes**
  - Pets: **Yes**

4. Yellow Banks Park Campground (Polk County)

- **Location**: 6801 SE 32nd Ave, Pleasant Hill, IA 50327
- **GPS Coordinates**: 41.5410° N, 93.4701° W
- **Website**: Yellow Banks Park
- **Amenities**:
  - Full Hookups: **Yes**
  - Electric: **50/30 AMP**
  - Water: **Yes**

◦ Pets: **Yes**

5. Prairie Rose State Park Campground (Shelby County)

- **Location**: 680 Rd M47, Harlan, IA 51537
- **GPS Coordinates**: 41.5884° N, 95.3174° W
- **Website**: Prairie Rose State Park
- **Amenities**:
  ◦ Full Hookups: **Yes**
  ◦ Electric: **50/30 AMP**
  ◦ Water: **Yes**
  ◦ Pets: **Yes**

6. Lake Red Rock Campground (Marion County)

- **Location**: 1105 N Hwy T15, Knoxville, IA 50138
- **GPS Coordinates**: 41.3622° N, 93.0779° W
- **Website**: Lake Red Rock Campground
- **Amenities**:
  ◦ Full Hookups: **No**
  ◦ Electric: **50/30 AMP**
  ◦ Water: **Yes**
  ◦ Pets: **Yes**

7. Brushy Creek State Recreation Area (Webster County)

- **Location**: 3175 Brushy Creek Rd, Lehigh, IA 50557
- **GPS Coordinates**: 42.3670° N, 93.9630° W
- **Website**: Brushy Creek State Recreation Area
- **Amenities**:
  ◦ Full Hookups: **Yes**
  ◦ Electric: **50/30 AMP**
  ◦ Water: **Yes**
  ◦ Pets: **Yes**

8. Jefferson County Park Campground (Jefferson County)

- **Location**: 2003 Libertyville Rd, Fairfield, IA 52556
- **GPS Coordinates**: 41.0072° N, 91.9857° W
- **Website**: Jefferson County Park
- **Amenities**:
  - Full Hookups: **No**
  - Electric: **30 AMP**
  - Water: **Yes**
  - Pets: **Yes**

KANSAS

County and Municipal RV Campgrounds in Kansas

1. Linn County Park & Marina (Linn County)

- **Location**: 23510 Valley Rd, La Cygne, KS 66040
- **GPS Coordinates**: 38.2947° N, 94.7369° W
- **Website**: Linn County Park & Marina
- **Amenities**:
  - Full Hookups: **Yes**
  - Electric: **50/30 AMP**
  - Water: **Yes**
  - Pets: **Yes**

2. Marion County Park & Lake (Marion County)

- **Location**: 1 Office Dr, Marion, KS 66861
- **GPS Coordinates**: 38.3643° N, 97.0877° W
- **Website**: Marion County Park & Lake
- **Amenities**:
  - Full Hookups: **Yes**
  - Electric: **50/30 AMP**
  - Water: **Yes**

○ Pets: **Yes**

KENTUCKY

County and Municipal RV Campgrounds in Kentucky

1. Jacobson Park Campground (Fayette County)

- **Location**: 4001 Athens Boonesboro Rd, Lexington, KY 40509
- **GPS Coordinates**: 37.9714° N, 84.4195° W
- **Website**: Jacobson Park
- **Amenities**:
  ○ Full Hookups: **No**
  ○ Electric: **30/20 AMP**
  ○ Water: **Yes**
  ○ Pets: **Yes**

2. A. J. Jolly Park (Campbell County)

- **Location**: 1501 Race Track Rd, Alexandria, KY 41001
- **GPS Coordinates**: 38.8789° N, 84.3737° W
- **Website**: A. J. Jolly Park
- **Amenities**:
  ○ Full Hookups: **Yes**
  ○ Electric: **50/30 AMP**
  ○ Water: **Yes**

3. Levi Jackson Wilderness Road Park (Laurel County)

- **Location: 998 Levi Jackson Mill Rd, London, KY 40744**
- **GPS Coordinates: 37.0944° N, 84.0608° W**
- **Website: Levi Jackson Wilderness Road Park**
- **Amenities:**
  ○ Full Hookups: Yes
  ○ **Electric: 50/30 AMP**

- Water: Yes
- Pets: Yes

LOUISIANNA

County and Municipal RV Campgrounds in Louisiana

1. Lafreniere Park (Jefferson Parish)

- Location: 3000 Downs Blvd, Metairie, LA 70003
- GPS Coordinates: 29.9975° N, 90.2262° W
- Website: Lafreniere Park
- Amenities:
  - Full Hookups: No
  - Electric: N/A
  - Water: No
  - Pets: Yes

MAINE

County and Municipal RV Campgrounds in Maine

1. Holbrook Island Sanctuary (Hancock County)

- Location: 172 Indian Bar Rd, Brooksville, ME 04617
- GPS Coordinates: 44.3500° N, 68.7983° W
- Website: Holbrook Island Sanctuary
- Amenities:
  - Full Hookups: No
  - Electric: None
  - Water: No
  - Pets: Yes

2. Hadley's Point Campground (Hancock County)

- **Location**: 33 Hadley Point Rd, Bar Harbor, ME 04609
- **GPS Coordinates**: 44.4371° N, 68.3083° W
- **Website**: Hadley's Point Campground
- **Amenities**:
  - Full Hookups: **Yes**
  - Electric: **50/30 AMP**
  - Water: **Yes**
  - Pets: **Yes**

3. Riverbend Campground (Oxford County)

- **Location**: 1540 Main St, Leeds, ME 04263
- **GPS Coordinates**: 44.3531° N, 70.1666° W
- **Website**: Riverbend Campground
- **Amenities**:
  - Full Hookups: **Yes**
  - Electric: **50/30 AMP**
  - Water: **Yes**
  - Pets: **Yes**

4. Bar Harbor Campground (Hancock County)

- **Location**: 409 ME-3, Bar Harbor, ME 04609
- **GPS Coordinates**: 44.4260° N, 68.2812° W
- **Website**: Bar Harbor Campground
- **Amenities**:
  - Full Hookups: **Yes**
  - Electric: **50/30 AMP**
  - Water: **Yes**
  - Pets: **Yes**

MARYLAND

1. Assateague Island National Seashore (Worcester County)

- **Location**: 7206 National Seashore Ln, Berlin, MD 21811
- **GPS Coordinates**: 38.0509° N, 75.2367° W
- **Website**: Assateague Island
- **Amenities**:
  - Full Hookups: **No**
  - Electric: **None**
  - Water: **No**
  - Pets: **Yes** (in certain areas)

MASSACHUSETTS

County and Municipal RV Campgrounds in Massachusetts

1. Salisbury Beach State Reservation (Essex County)

- **Location**: 1 Beach Rd, Salisbury, MA 01952
- **GPS Coordinates**: 42.8415° N, 70.8170° W
- **Website**: Salisbury Beach State Reservation
- **Amenities**:
  - Full Hookups: **Yes**
  - Electric: **50/30 AMP**
  - Water: **Yes**
  - Pets: **No**

2. Scusset Beach State Reservation (Plymouth County)

- **Location**: 20 Scusset Beach Rd, Sagamore Beach, MA 02562
- **GPS Coordinates**: 41.7796° N, 70.5097° W
- **Website**: Scusset Beach State Reservation
- **Amenities**:
  - Full Hookups: **Yes**

- Electric: **50/30 AMP**
- Water: **Yes**
- Pets: **No**

3. Shawme-Crowell State Forest (Barnstable County)

- **Location**: 42 Main St, Sandwich, MA 02563
- **GPS Coordinates**: 41.7201° N, 70.5143° W
- **Website**: Shawme-Crowell State Forest
- **Amenities**:
  - Full Hookups: **No**
  - Electric: **None**
  - Water: **Yes**
  - Pets: **Yes**

4. Myles Standish State Forest (Plymouth County)

- **Location**: 194 Cranberry Rd, Carver, MA 02330
- **GPS Coordinates**: 41.8300° N, 70.6835° W
- **Website**: Myles Standish State Forest
- **Amenities**:
  - Full Hookups: **No**
  - Electric: **None**
  - Water: **Yes**
  - Pets: **Yes**

5. Lorraine Park Campground (Hampden County)

- **Location**: 106 E Mountain Rd, Hampden, MA 01036
- **GPS Coordinates**: 42.0635° N, 72.4254° W
- **Website**: N/A (local municipal campground)
- **Amenities**:
  - Full Hookups: **No**
  - Electric: **None**
  - Water: **Yes**

- Pets: **Yes**

MICHIGAN

County and Municipal RV Campgrounds in Michigan

1. Traverse City State Park (Grand Traverse County)

- **Location**: 1132 US-31 N, Traverse City, MI 49686
- **GPS Coordinates**: 44.7441° N, 85.5559° W
- **Website**: Traverse City State Park
- **Amenities**:
  - Full Hookups: **No**
  - Electric: **50/30 AMP**
  - Water: **Yes**
  - Pets: **Yes**

2. Brighton Recreation Area (Livingston County)

- **Location**: 6360 Chilson Rd, Howell, MI 48843
- **GPS Coordinates**: 42.5186° N, 83.8492° W
- **Website**: Brighton Recreation Area
- **Amenities**:
  - Full Hookups: **No**
  - Electric: **50/30 AMP**
  - Water: **Yes**
  - Pets: **Yes**

3. Belle Isle Park (Wayne County)

- **Location**: Belle Isle Park, Detroit, MI 48207
- **GPS Coordinates**: 42.3454° N, 82.9716° W
- **Website**: Belle Isle Park
- **Amenities**:
  - Full Hookups: **No**

- Electric: **None**
- Water: **Yes**
- Pets: **Yes**

MINNESOTA

County and Municipal RV Campgrounds in Minnesota

1. Lake Elmo Park Reserve (Washington County)

- **Location**: 1515 Keats Ave N, Lake Elmo, MN 55042
- **GPS Coordinates**: 45.0033° N, 92.9022° W
- **Website**: Lake Elmo Park Reserve
- **Amenities**:
  - Full Hookups: **No**
  - Electric: **50/30 AMP**
  - Water: **Yes**
  - Pets: **Yes**

2. Lebanon Hills Regional Park (Dakota County)

- **Location**: 860 Cliff Rd, Eagan, MN 55123
- **GPS Coordinates**: 44.7892° N, 93.1705° W
- **Website**: Lebanon Hills Regional Park
- **Amenities**:
  - Full Hookups: **No**
  - Electric: **50/30 AMP**
  - Water: **Yes**
  - Pets: **Yes** (on leash)

3. Rice Creek Chain of Lakes Park Reserve (Anoka County)

- **Location**: 7401 Main St, Lino Lakes, MN 55038
- **GPS Coordinates**: 45.1931° N, 93.0867° W
- **Website**: Rice Creek Chain of Lakes Park

- **Amenities**:
  - Full Hookups: **No**
  - Electric: **50/30 AMP**
  - Water: **Yes**
  - Pets: **Yes**

4. Baker Park Reserve Campground (Hennepin County)

- **Location**: 2309 Baker Park Rd, Maple Plain, MN 55359
- **GPS Coordinates**: 45.0115° N, 93.6192° W
- **Website**: Baker Park Reserve Campground
- **Amenities**:
  - Full Hookups: **Yes**
  - Electric: **50/30 AMP**
  - Water: **Yes**
  - Pets: **Yes**

5. Lake Byllesby Regional Park (Dakota County)

- **Location**: 7650 Echo Point Rd, Cannon Falls, MN 55009
- **GPS Coordinates**: 44.4866° N, 92.9099° W
- **Website**: Lake Byllesby Regional Park
- **Amenities**:
  - Full Hookups: **Yes**
  - Electric: **50/30 AMP**
  - Water: **Yes**
  - Pets: **Yes** (on leash)

MISSISSIPPI

Additional County and Municipal RV Campgrounds in Mississippi

1. Lowndes County Sportsplex (Lowndes County)

- **Location**: 3147 Airport Rd, Columbus, MS 39701

- **GPS Coordinates**: 33.4834° N, 88.3953° W
- **Website**: Lowndes County Sportsplex
- **Amenities**:
  - Full Hookups: **Yes**
  - Electric: **50/30 AMP**
  - Water: **Yes**
  - Pets: **Yes**

2. Timberlake Campground (Hinds County)

- **Location**: 14234 U.S. 49, Brandon, MS 39047
- **GPS Coordinates**: 32.3964° N, 90.0364° W
- **Website**: Timberlake Campground
- **Amenities**:
  - Full Hookups: **Yes**
  - Electric: **50/30 AMP**
  - Water: **Yes**
  - Pets: **Yes**

3. Pascagoula Beach Park Campground (Jackson County)

- **Location**: 600 City Park St, Pascagoula, MS 39567
- **GPS Coordinates**: 30.3515° N, 88.5465° W
- **Website**: Pascagoula Beach Park
- **Amenities**:
  - Full Hookups: **Yes**
  - Electric: **50/30 AMP**
  - Water: **Yes**
  - Pets: **Yes**

4. Lamar Park (Lamar County)

- **Location**: 226 Pinewood Dr, Hattiesburg, MS 39402
- **GPS Coordinates**: 31.3195° N, 89.3952° W
- **Website**: Lamar County Parks

- **Amenities**:
  - Full Hookups: **No**
  - Electric: **50 AMP**
  - Water: **Yes**
  - Pets: **Yes**

5. Okatibbee Lake Campgrounds (Lauderdale County)

- **Location**: 9283 Pine Springs Rd, Meridian, MS 39305
- **GPS Coordinates**: 32.4866° N, 88.6671° W
- **Website**: Okatibbee Lake Campgrounds
- **Amenities**:
  - Full Hookups: **Yes**
  - Electric: **50/30 AMP**
  - Water: **Yes**
  - Pets: **Yes**

MISSOURI

County and Municipal RV Campgrounds in Missouri

None

MONTANA

County and Municipal RV Campgrounds in Montana

1. Lewis & Clark County Fairgrounds RV Park (Lewis & Clark County)

- **Location**: 98 W Custer Ave, Helena, MT 59602
- **GPS Coordinates**: 46.6175° N, 112.0362° W
- **Website**: Lewis & Clark County Fairgrounds RV Park
- **Amenities**:
  - Full Hookups: **Yes**
  - Electric: **50/30 AMP**

- Water: **Yes**
  - Pets: **Yes**

2. Yellowstone County Fairgrounds RV Park (Yellowstone County)

- **Location**: 308 6th Ave N, Billings, MT 59101
- **GPS Coordinates**: 45.7891° N, 108.5072° W
- **Website**: <u>Yellowstone County Fairgrounds</u>
- **Amenities**:
  - Full Hookups: **Yes**
  - Electric: **50/30 AMP**
  - Water: **Yes**
  - Pets: **Yes**

3. Flathead County Fairgrounds RV Park (Flathead County)

- **Location**: 265 N Meridian Rd, Kalispell, MT 59901
- **GPS Coordinates**: 48.2060° N, 114.3157° W
- **Website**: Flathead County Fairgrounds
- **Amenities**:
  - Full Hookups: **Yes**
  - Electric: **50/30 AMP**
  - Water: **Yes**
  - Pets: **Yes**

4. Missoula County Fairgrounds RV Park (Missoula County)

- **Location**: 1101 South Ave W, Missoula, MT 59801
- **GPS Coordinates**: 46.8565° N, 114.0266° W
- **Website**: <u>Missoula County Fairgrounds</u>
- **Amenities**:
  - Full Hookups: **Yes**
  - Electric: **50/30 AMP**
  - Water: **Yes**
  - Pets: **Yes**

5. **Valley County Fairgrounds RV Park (Valley County)**

- **Location**: 501 Court Square, Glasgow, MT 59230
- **GPS Coordinates**: 48.1963° N, 106.6334° W
- **Website**: Valley County Fairgrounds
- **Amenities**:
  - Full Hookups: **Yes**
  - Electric: **50/30 AMP**
  - Water: **Yes**
  - Pets: **Yes**

6. **Teton County RV Park (Teton County)**

- **Location: 720 N Main Ave, Choteau, MT 59422**
- **GPS Coordinates: 47.8145° N, 112.1845° W**
- **Website: Teton County RV Park**
- **Amenities:**
  - Full Hookups: Yes
  - Electric: 50/30 AMP
  - Water: Yes
  - Pets: Yes

7. **Powell County Fairgrounds RV Park (Powell County)**

- **Location: 500 Missouri Ave, Deer Lodge, MT 59722**
- **GPS Coordinates: 46.3933° N, 112.7292° W**
- **Website: Powell County Fairgrounds**
- **Amenities:**
  - Full Hookups: Yes
  - Electric: 50/30 AMP
  - Water: Yes
  - Pets: Yes

8. Sanders County Fairgrounds RV Park (Sanders County)

- Location: 30 River Rd W, Plains, MT 59859
- GPS Coordinates: 47.4693° N, 114.8981° W
- Website: Sanders County Fairgrounds
- Amenities:
  - Full Hookups: Yes
  - Electric: 50/30 AMP
  - Water: Yes
  - Pets: Yes

9. Libby City Park Campground (Lincoln County)

- Location: Flower St, Libby, MT 59923
- GPS Coordinates: 48.3915° N, 115.5545° W
- Website: Libby City Park Campground
- Amenities:
  - Full Hookups: No
  - Electric: 30 AMP
  - Water: Yes
  - Pets: Yes

NEBRASKA

County and Municipal RV Campgrounds in Nebraska

1. Two Rivers State Recreation Area (Douglas County)

- Location: 27702 F St, Waterloo, NE 68069
- GPS Coordinates: 41.2113° N, 96.3279° W
- Website: Two Rivers State Recreation Area
- Amenities:
  - Full Hookups: Yes
  - Electric: 50/30 AMP
  - Water: Yes

○ Pets: **Yes**

2. Fremont Lakes State Recreation Area (Dodge County)

- **Location**: 4349 W State Lakes Rd, Fremont, NE 68025
- **GPS Coordinates**: 41.4464° N, 96.5045° W
- **Website**: Fremont Lakes State Recreation Area
- **Amenities**:
  ○ Full Hookups: **No**
  ○ Electric: **50/30 AMP**
  ○ Water: **Yes**
  ○ Pets: **Yes**

3. Louisville State Recreation Area (Cass County)

- **Location**: 15810 NE-50, Louisville, NE 68037
- **GPS Coordinates**: 40.9975° N, 96.1621° W
- **Website**: Louisville State Recreation Area
- **Amenities**:
  ○ Full Hookups: **No**
  ○ Electric: **50/30 AMP**
  ○ Water: **Yes**
  ○ Pets: **Yes**

4. Fort Kearny State Recreation Area (Buffalo County)

- **Location**: 1020 V Rd, Kearney, NE 68847
- **GPS Coordinates**: 40.6735° N, 99.0341° W
- **Website**: Fort Kearny State Recreation Area
- **Amenities**:
  ○ Full Hookups: **No**
  ○ Electric: **50/30 AMP**
  ○ Water: **Yes**
  ○ Pets: **Yes**

5. Branched Oak State Recreation Area (Lancaster County)

- **Location**: 12000 W Branched Oak Rd, Raymond, NE 68428
- **GPS Coordinates**: 40.9863° N, 96.8256° W
- **Website**: Branched Oak State Recreation Area
- **Amenities**:
  - Full Hookups: **Yes**
  - Electric: **50/30 AMP**
  - Water: **Yes**
  - Pets: **Yes**

6. Lake McConaughy State Recreation Area (Keith County)

- **Location**: 1475 NE-61, Ogallala, NE 69153
- **GPS Coordinates**: 41.2458° N, 101.6505° W
- **Website**: Lake McConaughy State Recreation Area
- **Amenities**:
  - Full Hookups: **Yes**
  - Electric: **50/30 AMP**
  - Water: **Yes**
  - Pets: **Yes**

7. Rock Creek Station State Historical Park (Jefferson County)

- **Location**: 57426 710th Rd, Fairbury, NE 68352
- **GPS Coordinates**: 40.1208° N, 97.0465° W
- **Website**: Rock Creek Station State Historical Park
- **Amenities**:
  - Full Hookups: **No**
  - Electric: **50 AMP**
  - Water: **Yes**
  - Pets: **Yes**

NEVADA

County and Municipal RV Campgrounds in Nevada

1. Davis Creek Regional Park (Washoe County)

- **Location**: 25 Davis Creek Rd, Washoe Valley, NV 89704
- **GPS Coordinates**: 39.2842° N, 119.8183° W
- **Website**: Davis Creek Regional Park
- **Amenities**:
  - Full Hookups: **No**
  - Electric: **No**
  - Water: **Yes**
  - Pets: **Yes**

2. Lahontan State Recreation Area (Churchill and Lyon Counties)

- **Location**: 16799 Lahontan Dam Rd, Silver Springs, NV 89429
- **GPS Coordinates**: 39.4156° N, 119.0051° W
- **Website**: Lahontan State Recreation Area
- **Amenities**:
  - Full Hookups: **No**
  - Electric: **No**
  - Water: **No**
  - Pets: **Yes**

3. Boulder Beach Campground (Clark County)

- **Location: 268 Lakeshore Rd, Boulder City, NV 89005**
- **GPS Coordinates: 36.0505° N, 114.8049° W**
- **Website: Boulder Beach Campground**
- **Amenities:**
  - **Full Hookups: No**
  - **Electric: No**
  - **Water: Yes**

○ Pets: Yes

4. Wildhorse Reservoir State Recreation Area (Elko County)

- Location: NV-225, Owyhee, NV 89832
- GPS Coordinates: 41.6753° N, 115.7994° W
- Website: Wildhorse Reservoir SRA
- Amenities:
  ○ Full Hookups: No
  ○ Electric: No
  ○ Water: Yes
  ○ Pets: Yes

5. Rye Patch State Recreation Area (Pershing County)

- Location: Rye Patch Reservoir Rd, Lovelock, NV 89419
- GPS Coordinates: 40.5099° N, 118.2512° W
- Website: Rye Patch State Recreation Area
- Amenities:
  ○ Full Hookups: No
  ○ Electric: No
  ○ Water: Yes
  ○ Pets: Yes

6. Mesquite City RV Park (Clark County)

- Location: 202 W Mesquite Blvd, Mesquite, NV 89027
- GPS Coordinates: 36.8055° N, 114.0672° W
- Website: Mesquite City RV Park
- Amenities:
  ○ Full Hookups: Yes
  ○ Electric: 50/30 AMP
  ○ Water: Yes
  ○ Pets: Yes

NEW HAMPSHIRE

The campgrounds in New Hampshire typically offer partial services, and most parks are pet-friendly, though restrictions may apply in some areas. Only Ellacoya State Park and Hampton Beach State Park offer full hookups, while other parks offer varying amenities, including water and electric access.

NEW JERSEY

County and Municipal RV Campgrounds in New Jersey

1. Turkey Swamp Park (Monmouth County)

- **Location**: 200 Georgia Rd, Freehold, NJ 07728
- **GPS Coordinates**: 40.2145° N, 74.3077° W
- **Website**: Turkey Swamp Park
- **Amenities**:
  - Full Hookups: **No**
  - Electric: **20/30 AMP**
  - Water: **Yes**
  - Pets: **Yes**

2. Riverside County Park (Bergen County)

- **Location: 437 River Rd, North Arlington, NJ 07031**
- **GPS Coordinates: 40.7887° N, 74.1374° W**
- **Website: Bergen County Parks**
- **Amenities:**
  - **Full Hookups: No**
  - **Electric: No**
  - **Water: No**
  - **Pets: Yes**

3. Ocean County Park (Ocean County)

- Location: 659 Ocean Ave, Lakewood, NJ 08701
- GPS Coordinates: 40.1054° N, 74.2176° W
- Website: Ocean County Park
- Amenities:
  - Full Hookups: No
  - Electric: No
  - Water: Yes
  - Pets: Yes

4. Atsion Recreation Area (Burlington County)

- Location: 744 US-206, Shamong, NJ 08088
- GPS Coordinates: 39.7416° N, 74.7286° W
- Website: Wharton State Forest - Atsion
- Amenities:
  - Full Hookups: No
  - Electric: No
  - Water: Yes
  - Pets: Yes

5. Round Valley Recreation Area (Hunterdon County)

- Location: 1220 Lebanon-Stanton Rd, Lebanon, NJ 08833
- GPS Coordinates: 40.6334° N, 74.8295° W
- Website: Round Valley Recreation Area
- Amenities:
  - Full Hookups: No
  - Electric: No
  - Water: Yes
  - Pets: Yes

6. Spruce Run Recreation Area (Hunterdon County)

- Location: 68 Van Syckel's Rd, Clinton, NJ 08809
- GPS Coordinates: 40.6513° N, 74.9123° W
- Website: Spruce Run Recreation Area
- Amenities:
    - Full Hookups: No
    - Electric: No
    - Water: Yes
    - Pets: Yes

7. Mahlon Dickerson Reservation (Morris County)

- Location: 955 Weldon Rd, Jefferson, NJ 07849
- GPS Coordinates: 41.0109° N, 74.5871° W
- Website: Mahlon Dickerson Reservation
- Amenities:
    - Full Hookups: No
    - Electric: 30 AMP
    - Water: Yes
    - Pets: Yes

NEW MEXICO

1. Santa Fe County RV Park (Santa Fe County)

- Location: 97 Hale Rd, Santa Fe, NM 87508
- GPS Coordinates: 35.5849° N, 106.0775° W
- Website: Santa Fe County Parks
- Amenities:
    - Full Hookups: Yes
    - Electric: 50/30 AMP
    - Water: Yes
    - Pets: Yes

2. Carlsbad Beach Park (Eddy County)

- Location: 714 N. Canal St., Carlsbad, NM 88220
- GPS Coordinates: 32.4237° N, 104.2298° W
- Website: Carlsbad Parks & Recreation
- Amenities:
  - Full Hookups: No
  - Electric: 30 AMP
  - Water: Yes
  - Pets: Yes

3. Alameda Park Zoo RV Parking (City of Alamogordo)

- Location: 1021 N White Sands Blvd, Alamogordo, NM 88310
- GPS Coordinates: 32.9058° N, 105.9603° W
- Website: City of Alamogordo
- Amenities:
  - Full Hookups: No
  - Electric: No
  - Water: Yes
  - Pets: Yes

4. Riverside Park (San Juan County)

- Location: 500 S Light Plant Rd, Aztec, NM 87410
- GPS Coordinates: 36.8236° N, 107.9948° W
- Website: City of Aztec
- Amenities:
  - Full Hookups: No
  - Electric: No
  - Water: Yes
  - Pets: Yes

5. Lincoln County Fairgrounds (Lincoln County)

- Location: 501 E 5th St, Carrizozo, NM 88301
- GPS Coordinates: 33.6417° N, 105.8775° W
- Website: Lincoln County.
- Amenities:
  - Full Hookups: Yes
  - Electric: 50/30 AMP
  - Water: Yes
  - Pets: Yes

6. Farmington Riverside Nature Center (San Juan County)

- Location: 635 S. Murray Dr., Farmington, NM 87401
- GPS Coordinates: 36.7228° N, 108.1999° W
- Website: Farmington Parks
- Amenities:
  - Full Hookups: No
  - Electric: No
  - Water: Yes
  - Pets: Yes

7. Melrose City Park (Curry County)

- Location: Melrose, NM 88124
- GPS Coordinates: 34.4332° N, 103.6289° W
- Website: Curry County
- Amenities:
  - Full Hookups: No
  - Electric: No
  - Water: Yes
  - Pets: Yes

NEW YORK

County and Municipal RV Campgrounds in New York

1. Croton Point Park (Westchester County)

- **Location**: 1 Croton Point Ave, Croton-On-Hudson, NY 10520
- **GPS Coordinates**: 41.1878° N, 73.8901° W
- **Website**: Croton Point Park
- **Amenities**:
  - Full Hookups: **Yes**
  - Electric: **30/50 AMP**
  - Water: **Yes**
  - Pets: **Yes** (leashed)

2. Nickerson Beach Park (Nassau County)

- **Location**: 880 Lido Blvd, Lido Beach, NY 11561
- **GPS Coordinates**: 40.5885° N, 73.6383° W
- **Website**: Nickerson Beach Park
- **Amenities**:
  - Full Hookups: **Yes**
  - Electric: **50 AMP**
  - Water: **Yes**
  - Pets: **No**

3. Ulster County Fairgrounds (Ulster County)

- **Location**: 249 Libertyville Rd, New Paltz, NY 12561
- **GPS Coordinates**: 41.7298° N, 74.0828° W
- **Website**: Ulster County Fairgrounds
- **Amenities**:
  - Full Hookups: **Yes**
  - Electric: **30/50 AMP**

- Water: **Yes**
  - Pets: **Yes** (leashed)

NORTH CAROLINA

County and Municipal RV Campgrounds in North Carolina

1. Currituck County Rural Center (Currituck County)

- **Location**: 184 Milburn Sawyer Rd, Powells Point, NC 27966
- **GPS Coordinates**: 36.1657° N, 75.8501° W
- **Website**: Currituck County Rural Center
- **Amenities**:
  - Full Hookups: **Yes**
  - Electric: **50/30 AMP**
  - Water: **Yes**
  - Pets: **Yes**

2. Dan Nicholas Park Campground (Rowan County)

- **Location**: 6800 Bringle Ferry Rd, Salisbury, NC 28146
- **GPS Coordinates**: 35.6288° N, 80.3521° W
- **Website**: Dan Nicholas Park
- **Amenities**:
  - Full Hookups: **Yes**
  - Electric: **50/30 AMP**
  - Water: **Yes**
  - Pets: **Yes** (must be leashed)

3. Little Pee Dee Campground (Columbus County)

- **Location**: 129 Park Ln, Whiteville, NC 28472
- **GPS Coordinates**: 34.2815° N, 78.7410° W
- **Website**: Columbus County Parks
- **Amenities**:

- Full Hookups: **No**
- Electric: **30 AMP**
- Water: **Yes**
- Pets: **Yes**

4. Hagan-Stone Park Campground (Guilford County)

- **Location**: 5920 Hagan-Stone Park Rd, Pleasant Garden, NC 27313
- **GPS Coordinates**: 35.9301° N, 79.7328° W
- **Website**: Hagan-Stone Park
- **Amenities**:
  - Full Hookups: **Yes**
  - Electric: **30 AMP**
  - Water: **Yes**
  - Pets: **Yes**

5. Ebenezer Park (York County, near Charlotte area)

- **Location**: 4490 Boatshore Rd, Rock Hill, SC 29732
- **GPS Coordinates**: 35.0057° N, 81.0523° W
- **Website**: Ebenezer Park
- **Amenities**:
  - Full Hookups: **Yes**
  - Electric: **50/30 AMP**
  - Water: **Yes**
  - Pets: **Yes**

6. Mayo Park Campground (Person County)

- **Location**: 1013 Neal's Store Rd, Roxboro, NC 27574
- **GPS Coordinates**: 36.4922° N, 78.9756° W
- **Website**: Mayo Park
- **Amenities**:
  - Full Hookups: **No**

- Electric: **30 AMP**
- Water: **Yes**
- Pets: **Yes**

7. Jordan Lake County Park (Chatham County)

- **Location**: 280 State Park Rd, Apex, NC 27523
- **GPS Coordinates**: 35.7351° N, 79.0169° W
- **Website**: <u>Chatham County Parks</u>
- **Amenities**:
  - Full Hookups: **No**
  - Electric: **50/30 AMP**
  - Water: **Yes**
  - Pets: **Yes**

8. Lake Reidsville Campground (City of Reidsville)

- **Location: 630 Water Works Rd, Reidsville, NC 27320**
- **GPS Coordinates: 36.3645° N, 79.7126° W**
- **Website: Lake Reidsville**
- **Amenities:**
  - **Full Hookups: Yes**
  - **Electric: 50/30 AMP**
  - **Water: Yes**
  - **Pets: Yes**

9. Rolling View Campground (Durham County)

- **Location: 4201 Baptist Rd, Durham, NC 27703**
- **GPS Coordinates: 36.0125° N, 78.8073° W**
- **Website: <u>Rolling View Campground</u>**
- **Amenities:**
  - **Full Hookups: No**
  - **Electric: 30 AMP**
  - **Water: Yes**

o Pets: Yes

10. Davidson River Campground (Transylvania County)

- Location: 1 Davidson River Cir, Pisgah Forest, NC 28768
- GPS Coordinates: 35.2825° N, 82.7213° W
- Website: Davidson River Campground
- Amenities:
  - o Full Hookups: No
  - o Electric: 30 AMP
  - o Water: Yes
  - o Pets: Yes

11. Cane Creek Park (Union County)

- Location: 5213 Harkey Rd, Waxhaw, NC 28173
- GPS Coordinates: 34.8845° N, 80.7123° W
- Website: Cane Creek Park
- Amenities:
  - o Full Hookups: Yes
  - o Electric: 50/30 AMP
  - o Water: Yes
  - o Pets: Yes

12. Holly Point Campground (Wake County)

- Location: 14424 New Light Rd, Wake Forest, NC 27587
- GPS Coordinates: 36.0114° N, 78.6881° W
- Website: Holly Point Campground
- Amenities:
  - o Full Hookups: No
  - o Electric: 30 AMP
  - o Water: Yes
  - o Pets: Yes

13. Yates Mill County Park (Wake County)

- **Location: 4620 Lake Wheeler Rd, Raleigh, NC 27603**
- **GPS Coordinates: 35.7247° N, 78.7031° W**
- **Website: Yates Mill County Park**
- **Amenities:**
  - **Full Hookups: No**
  - **Electric: No**
  - **Water: Yes**
  - **Pets: Yes**

NORTH DAKOTA

County and Municipal RV Campgrounds in North Dakota

1. General Sibley Park and Campground (City of Bismarck)

- **Location**: 5001 S Washington St, Bismarck, ND 58504
- **GPS Coordinates**: 46.7589° N, 100.7961° W
- **Website**: General Sibley Park
- **Amenities:**
  - Full Hookups: **Yes**
  - Electric: **50/30 AMP**
  - Water: **Yes**
  - Pets: **Yes** (must be leashed)

2. Hillcrest Acres Campground (City of Jamestown)

- **Location**: 601 25th St SW, Jamestown, ND 58401
- **GPS Coordinates**: 46.8872° N, 98.7174° W
- **Website**: Hillcrest Acres Campground
- **Amenities:**
  - Full Hookups: **Yes**
  - Electric: **30 AMP**
  - Water: **Yes**

   ◦ Pets: **Yes**

3. Red River Valley Fair Campground (Cass County)

- **Location**: 1805 Main Ave W, West Fargo, ND 58078
- **GPS Coordinates**: 46.8741° N, 96.9168° W
- **Website**: <u>Red River Valley Fair</u>
- **Amenities**:
  - ◦ Full Hookups: **Yes**
  - ◦ Electric: **50/30 AMP**
  - ◦ Water: **Yes**
  - ◦ Pets: **Yes** (must be leashed)

4. Fort Ransom Village Campground (Ransom County)

- **Location**: 101 Ash St, Fort Ransom, ND 58033
- **GPS Coordinates**: 46.5272° N, 97.9253° W
- **Website**: <u>Fort Ransom Village</u>
- **Amenities**:
  - ◦ Full Hookups: **No**
  - ◦ Electric: **30 AMP**
  - ◦ Water: **Yes**
  - ◦ Pets: **Yes**

5. Turtle River Campground (Grand Forks County)

- **Location**: 3084 Park Ave NE, Arvilla, ND 58214
- **GPS Coordinates**: 47.9236° N, 97.4908° W
- **Website**: <u>Turtle River Campground</u>
- **Amenities**:
  - ◦ Full Hookups: **No**
  - ◦ Electric: **30 AMP**
  - ◦ Water: **Yes**
  - ◦ Pets: **Yes**

6. City of Minot Campground (Ward County)

- **Location**: 1001 31st Ave SE, Minot, ND 58701
- **GPS Coordinates**: 48.2158° N, 101.2781° W
- **Website**: City of Minot Parks
- **Amenities**:
  - Full Hookups: **No**
  - Electric: **30 AMP**
  - Water: **Yes**
  - Pets: **Yes**

7. Devils Lake City Park Campground (Ramsey County)

- Location: 1209 Hwy 20 S, Devils Lake, ND 58301
- GPS Coordinates: 48.1120° N, 98.8658° W
- Website: Devils Lake City Campground
- Amenities:
  - Full Hookups: Yes
  - Electric: 50/30 AMP
  - Water: Yes
  - Pets: Yes (leashed)

8. Icelandic State Park (Pembina County)

- Location: 13571 Hwy 5, Cavalier, ND 58220
- GPS Coordinates: 48.8673° N, 97.6225° W
- Website: Icelandic State Park
- Amenities:
  - Full Hookups: No
  - Electric: 30 AMP
  - Water: Yes
  - Pets: Yes

Note: Although this is labeled a state park, some sections may be municipally managed.

9. Steele City Park Campground (Kidder County)

- Location: 204 Mitchell Ave N, Steele, ND 58482
- GPS Coordinates: 46.8551° N, 99.9168° W
- Website: City of Steele
- Amenities:
  - Full Hookups: No
  - Electric: 30 AMP
  - Water: Yes
  - Pets: Yes

10. Hazen Bay Recreation Area (Mercer County)

- Location: 928 County Rd 37, Hazen, ND 58545
- GPS Coordinates: 47.2992° N, 101.6237° W
- Website: Hazen Bay Recreation
- Amenities:
  - Full Hookups: Yes
  - Electric: 50/30 AMP
  - Water: Yes
  - Pets: Yes

11. New Rockford City Park Campground (Eddy County)

- Location: 327 1st Ave N, New Rockford, ND 58356
- GPS Coordinates: 47.6789° N, 99.1376° W
- Website: New Rockford Parks
- Amenities:
  - Full Hookups: No
  - Electric: 30 AMP
  - Water: Yes
  - Pets: Yes

OHIO

County and Municipal RV Campgrounds in Ohio

1. Butler County Fairgrounds (Butler County)

- **Location**: 1715 Fairgrove Ave, Hamilton, OH 45011
- **GPS Coordinates**: 39.4171° N, 84.5743° W
- **Website**: Butler County Fairgrounds
- **Amenities**:
  - Full Hookups: **Yes**
  - Electric: **50/30 AMP**
  - Water: **Yes**
  - Pets: **Yes** (must be leashed)

2. Lakeview Park Campground (Lorain County)

- **Location**: 1800 W Erie Ave, Lorain, OH 44052
- **GPS Coordinates**: 41.4712° N, 82.1931° W
- **Website**: Lakeview Park
- **Amenities**:
  - Full Hookups: **No**
  - Electric: **30 AMP**
  - Water: **Yes**
  - Pets: **Yes**

3. Geauga County Fairgrounds (Geauga County)

- **Location**: 14373 N Cheshire St, Burton, OH 44021
- **GPS Coordinates**: 41.4731° N, 81.1454° W
- **Website**: Geauga County Fairgrounds
- **Amenities**:
  - Full Hookups: **No**
  - Electric: **30 AMP**
  - Water: **Yes**

○ Pets: **Yes**

4. Erie County Fairgrounds (Erie County)

- **Location**: 3110 Columbus Ave, Sandusky, OH 44870
- **GPS Coordinates**: 41.4281° N, 82.7217° W
- **Website**: Erie County Fairgrounds
- **Amenities**:
  ○ Full Hookups: **Yes**
  ○ Electric: **50/30 AMP**
  ○ Water: **Yes**
  ○ Pets: **Yes**

5. Richland County Fairgrounds (Richland County)

- **Location**: 750 N Home Rd, Mansfield, OH 44906
- **GPS Coordinates**: 40.7793° N, 82.5471° W
- **Website**: Richland County Fairgrounds
- **Amenities**:
  ○ Full Hookups: **Yes**
  ○ Electric: **30 AMP**
  ○ Water: **Yes**
  ○ Pets: **Yes**

6. Medina County Fairgrounds (Medina County)

- **Location**: 720 W Smith Rd, Medina, OH 44256
- **GPS Coordinates**: 41.1364° N, 81.8712° W
- **Website**: Medina County Fairgrounds
- **Amenities**:
  ○ Full Hookups: **No**
  ○ Electric: **30 AMP**
  ○ Water: **Yes**
  ○ Pets: **Yes**

7. Hamilton County Park District - Winton Woods Campground

- **Location**: 10245 Winton Rd, Cincinnati, OH 45231
- **GPS Coordinates**: 39.2647° N, 84.5228° W
- **Website**: Winton Woods Campground
- **Amenities**:
  - Full Hookups: **Yes**
  - Electric: **50/30 AMP**
  - Water: **Yes**
  - Pets: **Yes**

8. Summit County Fairgrounds (Summit County)

- **Location**: 229 E Howe Rd, Tallmadge, OH 44278
- **GPS Coordinates**: 41.1017° N, 81.4322° W
- **Website**: Summit County Fairgrounds
- **Amenities**:
  - Full Hookups: **No**
  - Electric: **30 AMP**
  - Water: **Yes**
  - Pets: **Yes**

9. Lorain County Metro Parks - Findley Lake Campground

- **Location: 25381 State Route 58, Wellington, OH 44090**
- **GPS Coordinates: 41.1411° N, 82.2288° W**
- **Website: Findley Lake Campground**
- **Amenities:**
  - **Full Hookups: No**
  - **Electric: 30 AMP**
  - **Water: Yes**
  - **Pets: Yes**

10. Van Wert County Fairgrounds (Van Wert County)

- Location: 1055 S Washington St, Van Wert, OH 45891
- GPS Coordinates: 40.8587° N, 84.5839° W
- Website: Van Wert County Fairgrounds
- Amenities:
  - Full Hookups: Yes
  - Electric: 50/30 AMP
  - Water: Yes
  - Pets: Yes

11. Auglaize County Fairgrounds (Auglaize County)

- Location: 1001 Fairview Dr, Wapakoneta, OH 45895
- GPS Coordinates: 40.5703° N, 84.1828° W
- Website: Auglaize County Fairgrounds
- Amenities:
  - Full Hookups: No
  - Electric: 30 AMP
  - Water: Yes
  - Pets: Yes

12. Fairfield County Fairgrounds (Fairfield County)

- Location: 157 E Fair Ave, Lancaster, OH 43130
- GPS Coordinates: 39.7159° N, 82.5952° W
- Website: Fairfield County Fairgrounds
- Amenities:
  - Full Hookups: No
  - Electric: 30 AMP
  - Water: Yes
  - Pets: Yes

13. Wood County Fairgrounds (Wood County)

- Location: 13800 W Poe Rd, Bowling Green, OH 43402
- GPS Coordinates: 41.3897° N, 83.6682° W
- Website: Wood County Fairgrounds
- Amenities:
  - Full Hookups: No
  - Electric: 30 AMP
  - Water: Yes
  - Pets: Yes

14. Ottawa County Fairgrounds (Ottawa County)

- Location: 7870 W State Route 163, Oak Harbor, OH 43449
- GPS Coordinates: 41.5079° N, 83.1556° W
- Website: Ottawa County Fairgrounds
- Amenities:
  - Full Hookups: No
  - Electric: 30 AMP
  - Water: Yes
  - Pets: Yes

15. Coshocton County Fairgrounds (Coshocton County)

- Location: 707 Kenilworth Ave, Coshocton, OH 43812
- GPS Coordinates: 40.2694° N, 81.8682° W
- Website: Coshocton County Fairgrounds
- Amenities:
  - Full Hookups: No
  - Electric: 30 AMP
  - Water: Yes
  - Pets: Yes

OKLAHOMA

County and Municipal RV Campgrounds in Oklahoma

1. Cleveland County Fairgrounds (Cleveland County)

- **Location**: 615 E Robinson St, Norman, OK 73071
- **GPS Coordinates**: 35.2278° N, 97.4295° W
- **Website**: Cleveland County Fairgrounds
- **Amenities**:
    - Full Hookups: **Yes**
    - Electric: **50/30 AMP**
    - Water: **Yes**
    - Pets: **Yes**

2. Canadian County Fairgrounds (Canadian County)

- **Location**: 220 N Country Club Rd, El Reno, OK 73036
- **GPS Coordinates**: 35.5369° N, 97.9753° W
- **Website**: Canadian County Fairgrounds
- **Amenities**:
    - Full Hookups: **Yes**
    - Electric: **50/30 AMP**
    - Water: **Yes**
    - Pets: **Yes**

3. Tulsa County Fairgrounds (Tulsa Expo Square)

- **Location**: 4145 E 21st St, Tulsa, OK 74114
- **GPS Coordinates**: 36.1355° N, 95.9369° W
- **Website**: Tulsa Expo Square
- **Amenities**:
    - Full Hookups: **Yes**
    - Electric: **50/30 AMP**
    - Water: **Yes**

    ○ Pets: **Yes**

4. Rogers County Fairgrounds (Rogers County)

- **Location**: 400 Veterans Pkwy, Claremore, OK 74017
- **GPS Coordinates**: 36.3192° N, 95.6058° W
- **Website**: <u>Rogers County Fairgrounds</u>
- **Amenities**:
  - ○ Full Hookups: **No**
  - ○ Electric: **30 AMP**
  - ○ Water: **Yes**
  - ○ Pets: **Yes**

5. Pottawatomie County Fairgrounds (Pottawatomie County)

- **Location**: 401 N Bell Ave, Shawnee, OK 74801
- **GPS Coordinates**: 35.3334° N, 96.9247° W
- **Website**: <u>Pottawatomie County Fairgrounds</u>
- **Amenities**:
  - ○ Full Hookups: **No**
  - ○ Electric: **30 AMP**
  - ○ Water: **Yes**
  - ○ Pets: **Yes**

6. Grady County Fairgrounds (Grady County)

- **Location**: 500 E Choctaw Ave, Chickasha, OK 73018
- **GPS Coordinates**: 35.0515° N, 97.9359° W
- **Website**: <u>Grady County Fairgrounds</u>
- **Amenities**:
  - ○ Full Hookups: **Yes**
  - ○ Electric: **50/30 AMP**
  - ○ Water: **Yes**
  - ○ Pets: **Yes**

7. Wagoner Civic Center Campground (Wagoner County)

- **Location**: 301 S Grant Ave, Wagoner, OK 74467
- **GPS Coordinates**: 35.9567° N, 95.3705° W
- **Website**: Wagoner Civic Center
- **Amenities**:
  - Full Hookups: **No**
  - Electric: **30 AMP**
  - Water: **Yes**
  - Pets: **Yes**

8. Payne County Expo Center (Payne County)

- **Location: 4518 Expo Cir E, Stillwater, OK 74075**
- **GPS Coordinates: 36.1387° N, 97.0561° W**
- **Website: Payne County Expo Center**
- **Amenities:**
  - Full Hookups: Yes
  - Electric: 50/30 AMP
  - Water: Yes
  - Pets: Yes

9. Washington County Fairgrounds (Washington County)

- **Location: 1109 N Delaware St, Dewey, OK 74029**
- **GPS Coordinates: 36.7981° N, 95.9356° W**
- **Website: Washington County Fairgrounds**
- **Amenities:**
  - Full Hookups: No
  - Electric: 30 AMP
  - Water: Yes
  - Pets: Yes

10. Garfield County Fairgrounds (Garfield County)

- Location: 111 W Purdue Ave, Enid, OK 73701
- GPS Coordinates: 36.4332° N, 97.8784° W
- Website: <u>Garfield County Fairgrounds</u>
- Amenities:
  - Full Hookups: Yes
  - Electric: 50/30 AMP
  - Water: Yes
  - Pets: Yes

11. Kay County Fairgrounds (Kay County)

- Location: 800 S Main St, Blackwell, OK 74631
- GPS Coordinates: 36.8004° N, 97.2826° W
- Website: <u>Kay County Fairgrounds</u>
- Amenities:
  - Full Hookups: No
  - Electric: 30 AMP
  - Water: Yes
  - Pets: Yes

12. McClain County Expo Center (McClain County)

- Location: 1715 Hardcastle Blvd, Purcell, OK 73080
- GPS Coordinates: 35.0164° N, 97.3725° W
- Website: <u>McClain County Expo Center</u>
- Amenities:
  - Full Hookups: Yes
  - Electric: 50/30 AMP
  - Water: Yes
  - Pets: Yes

13. Creek County Fairgrounds (Creek County)

- Location: 17808 OK-66, Kellyville, OK 74039
- GPS Coordinates: 35.9481° N, 96.2195° W
- Website: <u>Creek County Fairgrounds</u>
- Amenities:
  - Full Hookups: No
  - Electric: 30 AMP
  - Water: Yes
  - Pets: Yes

OREGON

County and Municipal RV Campgrounds in Oregon

1. Clackamas County Fairgrounds & Event Center (Clackamas County)

- Location: 694 NE 4th Ave, Canby, OR 97013
- GPS Coordinates: 45.2667° N, 122.6916° W
- Website: <u>Clackamas County Fairgrounds</u>
- Amenities:
  - Full Hookups: **Yes**
  - Electric: **50/30 AMP**
  - Water: **Yes**
  - Pets: **Yes** (leashed)

2. Deschutes County Fair & Expo Center (Deschutes County)

- Location: 3800 SW Airport Way, Redmond, OR 97756
- GPS Coordinates: 44.2438° N, 121.1629° W
- Website: Deschutes County Fair & Expo
- Amenities:
  - Full Hookups: **Yes**
  - Electric: **50/30 AMP**

- o Water: **Yes**
- o Pets: **Yes**

3. Hood River County Fairgrounds (Hood River County)

- **Location**: 3020 Wy'East Rd, Hood River, OR 97031
- **GPS Coordinates**: 45.6822° N, 121.5372° W
- **Website**: Hood River Fairgrounds
- **Amenities**:
  - o Full Hookups: **No**
  - o Electric: **30 AMP**
  - o Water: **Yes**
  - o Pets: **Yes**

4. Benton County Fairgrounds (Benton County)

- **Location**: 110 SW 53rd St, Corvallis, OR 97333
- **GPS Coordinates**: 44.5412° N, 123.3127° W
- **Website**: Benton County Fairgrounds
- **Amenities**:
  - o Full Hookups: **Yes**
  - o Electric: **50/30 AMP**
  - o Water: **Yes**
  - o Pets: **Yes**

5. Jackson County Expo Park (Jackson County)

- **Location**: 1 Peninger Rd, Central Point, OR 97502
- **GPS Coordinates**: 42.3869° N, 122.9217° W
- **Website**: Jackson County Expo
- **Amenities**:
  - o Full Hookups: **Yes**
  - o Electric: **50/30 AMP**
  - o Water: **Yes**
  - o Pets: **Yes**

6. Lane County Fairgrounds (Lane County)

- **Location**: 796 W 13th Ave, Eugene, OR 97402
- **GPS Coordinates**: 44.0489° N, 123.1101° W
- **Website**: Lane County Fairgrounds
- **Amenities**:
  - Full Hookups: **No**
  - Electric: **30 AMP**
  - Water: **Yes**
  - Pets: **Yes**

7. Linn County Fair & Expo Center (Linn County)

- **Location**: 3700 Knox Butte Rd E, Albany, OR 97322
- **GPS Coordinates**: 44.6395° N, 123.0495° W
- **Website**: Linn County Fair & Expo
- **Amenities**:
  - Full Hookups: **Yes**
  - Electric: **50/30 AMP**
  - Water: **Yes**
  - Pets: **Yes**

8. Polk County Fairgrounds (Polk County)

- **Location**: 520 S Pacific Hwy W, Rickreall, OR 97371
- **GPS Coordinates**: 44.9271° N, 123.2154° W
- **Website**: Polk County Fairgrounds
- **Amenities**:
  - Full Hookups: **No**
  - Electric: **30 AMP**
  - Water: **Yes**
  - Pets: **Yes**

9. Josephine County Fairgrounds (Josephine County)

- Location: 1451 Fairgrounds Rd, Grants Pass, OR 97527
- GPS Coordinates: 42.4274° N, 123.3314° W
- Website: Josephine County Fairgrounds
- Amenities:
  - Full Hookups: Yes
  - Electric: 50/30 AMP
  - Water: Yes
  - Pets: Yes

10. Douglas County Fairgrounds (Douglas County)

- Location: 2110 Frear St, Roseburg, OR 97471
- GPS Coordinates: 43.2077° N, 123.3631° W
- Website: Douglas County Fairgrounds
- Amenities:
  - Full Hookups: Yes
  - Electric: 50/30 AMP
  - Water: Yes
  - Pets: Yes

11. Harney County Fairgrounds (Harney County)

- Location: 69660 S Egan Ave, Burns, OR 97720
- GPS Coordinates: 43.5889° N, 119.0586° W
- Website: Harney County Fairgrounds
- Amenities:
  - Full Hookups: No
  - Electric: 30 AMP
  - Water: Yes
  - Pets: Yes

12. Tillamook County Fairgrounds (Tillamook County)

- Location: 4603 3rd St, Tillamook, OR 97141
- GPS Coordinates: 45.4567° N, 123.8427° W
- Website: <u>Tillamook County Fairgrounds</u>
- Amenities:
  - Full Hookups: No
  - Electric: 30 AMP
  - Water: Yes
  - Pets: Yes

13. Umatilla County Fairgrounds (Umatilla County)

- Location: 1705 E Airport Rd, Hermiston, OR 97838
- GPS Coordinates: 45.8393° N, 119.2803° W
- Website: <u>Umatilla County Fairgrounds</u>
- Amenities:
  - Full Hookups: No
  - Electric: 30 AMP
  - Water: Yes
  - Pets: Yes

PENNSYLVANIA

County and Municipal RV Campgrounds in Pennsylvania

1. Lancaster County Park (Lancaster County)

- Location: 1050 Rockford Rd, Lancaster, PA 17602
- GPS Coordinates: 40.0196° N, 76.2882° W
- Website: Lancaster County Parks
- Amenities:
  - Full Hookups: **Yes**
  - Electric: **30/50 AMP**
  - Water: **Yes**

o Pets: **Yes** (leashed)

2. Bucks County Park - Peace Valley Park (Bucks County)

- **Location**: 230 Creek Rd, Doylestown, PA 18901
- **GPS Coordinates**: 40.3367° N, 75.1703° W
- **Website**: Bucks County Parks
- **Amenities**:
  - Full Hookups: **No**
  - Electric: **30 AMP**
  - Water: **Yes**
  - Pets: **Yes**

3. Mifflin County Youth Park (Mifflin County)

- **Location**: 110 W Logan St, Reedsville, PA 17084
- **GPS Coordinates**: 40.6781° N, 77.5962° W
- **Website**: Mifflin County Youth Park
- **Amenities**:
  - Full Hookups: **Yes**
  - Electric: **30/50 AMP**
  - Water: **Yes**
  - Pets: **Yes**

4. Washington County Fairgrounds (Washington County)

- **Location**: 2151 N Main St, Washington, PA 15301
- **GPS Coordinates**: 40.1931° N, 80.2465° W
- **Website**: Washington County Fair
- **Amenities**:
  - Full Hookups: **Yes**
  - Electric: **30/50 AMP**
  - Water: **Yes**
  - Pets: **Yes**

5. Montgomery County 4-H Center (Montgomery County)

- **Location**: 1015 Bridge Rd, Collegeville, PA 19426
- **GPS Coordinates**: 40.1995° N, 75.4256° W
- **Website**: Montgomery County 4-H Center
- **Amenities**:
  - Full Hookups: **No**
  - Electric: **30 AMP**
  - Water: **Yes**
  - Pets: **Yes**

6. Lycoming County Fairgrounds (Lycoming County)

- **Location**: 1 E Park St, Hughesville, PA 17737
- **GPS Coordinates**: 41.2415° N, 76.7267° W
- **Website**: <u>Lycoming County Fairgrounds</u>
- **Amenities**:
  - Full Hookups: **Yes**
  - Electric: **30/50 AMP**
  - Water: **Yes**
  - Pets: **Yes**

7. Westmoreland Fairgrounds (Westmoreland County)

- **Location**: 123 Blue Ribbon Ln, Greensburg, PA 15601
- **GPS Coordinates**: 40.2924° N, 79.4620° W
- **Website**: <u>Westmoreland Fairgrounds</u>
- **Amenities**:
  - Full Hookups: **Yes**
  - Electric: **30/50 AMP**
  - Water: **Yes**
  - Pets: **Yes**

8. York County Fairgrounds (York County)

- Location: 334 Carlisle Ave, York, PA 17404
- GPS Coordinates: 39.9554° N, 76.7512° W
- Website: York County Fair
- Amenities:
  - Full Hookups: No
  - Electric: 30 AMP
  - Water: Yes
  - Pets: Yes

9. Schuylkill County Fairgrounds (Schuylkill County)

- Location: 2270 Fair Rd, Schuylkill Haven, PA 17972
- GPS Coordinates: 40.6068° N, 76.1523° W
- Website: Schuylkill County Fair
- Amenities:
  - Full Hookups: No
  - Electric: 30 AMP
  - Water: Yes
  - Pets: Yes

10. Crawford County Fairgrounds (Crawford County)

- Location: 13291 Dickson Rd, Meadville, PA 16335
- GPS Coordinates: 41.6326° N, 80.1634° W
- Website: Crawford County Fairgrounds
- Amenities:
  - Full Hookups: No
  - Electric: 30 AMP
  - Water: Yes
  - Pets: Yes

11. Greene County Fairgrounds (Greene County)

- Location: 107 Fairgrounds Rd, Waynesburg, PA 15370
- GPS Coordinates: 39.9002° N, 80.1706° W
- Website: Greene County Fair
- Amenities:
  - Full Hookups: No
  - Electric: 30 AMP
  - Water: Yes
  - Pets: Yes

12. Lebanon Area Fairgrounds (Lebanon County)

- Location: 80 Rocherty Rd, Lebanon, PA 17042
- GPS Coordinates: 40.3120° N, 76.4297° W
- Website: Lebanon Area Fairgrounds
- Amenities:
  - Full Hookups: No
  - Electric: 30 AMP
  - Water: Yes
  - Pets: Yes

13. Clearfield County Fairgrounds (Clearfield County)

- Location: 5615 Park St, Clearfield, PA 16830
- GPS Coordinates: 41.0181° N, 78.4406° W
- Website: Clearfield County Fair
- Amenities:
  - Full Hookups: No
  - Electric: 30 AMP
  - Water: Yes
  - Pets: Yes

14. Fayette County Fairgrounds (Fayette County)

- Location: 132 Pechin Rd, Dunbar, PA 15431
- GPS Coordinates: 39.9774° N, 79.6028° W
- Website: <u>Fayette County Fair</u>
- Amenities:
  - Full Hookups: Yes
  - Electric: 50/30 AMP
  - Water: Yes
  - Pets: Yes

RHODE ISLAND

County and Municipal RV Campgrounds in Rhode Island

1. Melville Ponds Campground (Portsmouth, RI)

- Location: 181 Bradford Ave, Portsmouth, RI 02871
- GPS Coordinates: 41.5693° N, 71.2733° W
- Website: Melville Ponds Campground
- Amenities:
  - Full Hookups: Yes
  - Electric: 30/50 AMP
  - Water: Yes
  - Pets: Yes (leashed)

2. Burlingame State Park Campground – Charlestown Town Camping Area

- Location: 1 Burlingame State Park Rd, Charlestown, RI 02813 (Municipal-run area within a larger state park)
- GPS Coordinates: 41.3697° N, 71.6964° W
- Website: Charlestown Town Camping
- Amenities:
  - Full Hookups: No

- Electric: **30 AMP**
- Water: **Yes**
- Pets: **Yes** (restricted areas)

SOUTH CAROLINA

County and Municipal RV Campgrounds in South Carolina

1. Barnwell County RV Park (Barnwell County)

- **Location**: 155 Wall St, Barnwell, SC 29812
- **GPS Coordinates**: 33.2442° N, 81.3585° W
- **Website**: Barnwell County RV Park
- **Amenities**:
  - Full Hookups: **Yes**
  - Electric: **30/50 AMP**
  - Water: **Yes**
  - Pets: **Yes** (leashed)

2. Anderson Sports & Entertainment Center (Anderson County)

- **Location**: 3027 Martin Luther King Jr Blvd, Anderson, SC 29625
- **GPS Coordinates**: 34.5146° N, 82.6835° W
- **Website**: Anderson County Parks
- **Amenities**:
  - Full Hookups: **Yes**
  - Electric: **30/50 AMP**
  - Water: **Yes**
  - Pets: **Yes**

3. Horry County Recreation Parks (Horry County)

- **Location**: Various parks in Horry County, including the Myrtle Beach area

- **GPS Coordinates**: 33.7668° N, 78.9180° W (approx.)
- **Website**: Horry County Parks
- **Amenities**:
  - Full Hookups: **No** (some parks may have partial)
  - Electric: **30 AMP**
  - Water: **Yes**
  - Pets: **Yes** (specific rules apply)

4. Colleton County Recreation Center (Colleton County)

- **Location**: 280 Recreation Ln, Walterboro, SC 29488
- **GPS Coordinates**: 32.9150° N, 80.6663° W
- **Website**: Colleton County Recreation
- **Amenities**:
  - Full Hookups: **No**
  - Electric: **30 AMP**
  - Water: **Yes**
  - Pets: **Yes**

5. Spartanburg County Parks - Cleveland Park RV Sites (Spartanburg County)

- **Location**: 141 N Cleveland Park Dr, Spartanburg, SC 29303
- **GPS Coordinates**: 34.9454° N, 81.9147° W
- **Website**: Spartanburg County Parks
- **Amenities**:
  - Full Hookups: **No**
  - Electric: **30 AMP**
  - Water: **Yes**
  - Pets: **Yes**

6. James Island County Park (Charleston County)

- **Location**: 871 Riverland Dr, Charleston, SC 29412
- **GPS Coordinates**: 32.7357° N, 79.9773° W

- **Website**: James Island County Park
- **Amenities**:
  - Full Hookups: **Yes**
  - Electric: **30/50 AMP**
  - Water: **Yes**
  - Pets: **Yes** (with rules)

7. Georgetown County Parks - Carroll A. Campbell Marine Complex (Georgetown County)

- **Location**: 101 Riverwalk Dr, Georgetown, SC 29440
- **GPS Coordinates**: 33.3674° N, 79.2814° W
- **Website**: Georgetown County Parks
- **Amenities**:
  - Full Hookups: **No**
  - Electric: **30/50 AMP**
  - Water: **Yes**
  - Pets: **Yes**

8. Richland County Recreation Commission - Sesquicentennial State Park Area (Richland County)

- **Location**: 9564 Two Notch Rd, Columbia, SC 29223 (municipal-run area nearby)
- **GPS Coordinates**: 34.0755° N, 80.8871° W
- **Website**: Richland County Parks
- **Amenities**:
  - Full Hookups: **No**
  - Electric: **30 AMP**
  - Water: **Yes**
  - Pets: **Yes** (on leash)

9. Aiken County Parks - Boyd Pond Park (Aiken County)

- **Location**: 373 Boyd Pond Rd, Aiken, SC 29803
- **GPS Coordinates**: 33.4864° N, 81.7206° W
- **Website**: Aiken County Parks
- **Amenities**:
  - Full Hookups: **No**
  - Electric: **30 AMP**
  - Water: **Yes**
  - Pets: **Yes**

10. Florence County Parks - Lynches River County Park (Florence County)

- **Location**: 5094 County Park Rd, Coward, SC 29530
- **GPS Coordinates**: 33.9678° N, 79.7487° W
- **Website**: Florence County Parks
- **Amenities**:
  - Full Hookups: **No**
  - Electric: **30 AMP**
  - Water: **Yes**
  - Pets: **Yes**

11. Berkeley County Parks - Cypress Gardens RV Area (Berkeley County)

- **Location**: 3030 Cypress Gardens Rd, Moncks Corner, SC 29461
- **GPS Coordinates**: 33.0523° N, 79.9063° W
- **Website**: Berkeley County Parks
- **Amenities**:
  - Full Hookups: **No**
  - Electric: **30 AMP**
  - Water: **Yes**
  - Pets: **Yes**

SOUTH DAKOTA

County and Municipal RV Campgrounds in South Dakota

1. Pennington County Fairgrounds RV Park (Pennington County)

- **Location**: 800 San Francisco St, Rapid City, SD 57701
- **GPS Coordinates**: 44.0866° N, 103.2131° W
- **Website**: Pennington County Fairgrounds
- **Amenities**:
  - Full Hookups: **Yes**
  - Electric: **30/50 AMP**
  - Water: **Yes**
  - Pets: **Yes** (leashed)

2. Brown County Fairgrounds (Brown County)

- **Location**: 400 24th Ave NW, Aberdeen, SD 57401
- **GPS Coordinates**: 45.4737° N, 98.4852° W
- **Website**: Brown County Fairgrounds
- **Amenities**:
  - Full Hookups: **No**
  - Electric: **30 AMP**
  - Water: **Yes**
  - Pets: **Yes**

3. Yankton County 4-H Grounds (Yankton County)

- **Location**: 905 Whiting Dr, Yankton, SD 57078
- **GPS Coordinates**: 42.8770° N, 97.3974° W
- **Website**: Yankton County 4-H
- **Amenities**:
  - Full Hookups: **No**
  - Electric: **30 AMP**
  - Water: **Yes**

○ Pets: **Yes** (with rules)

4. Davison County Fairgrounds RV Park (Davison County)

- **Location**: 3200 W Havens St, Mitchell, SD 57301
- **GPS Coordinates**: 43.7094° N, 98.0480° W
- **Website**: Davison County Fairgrounds
- **Amenities**:
  ○ Full Hookups: **No**
  ○ Electric: **30 AMP**
  ○ Water: **Yes**
  ○ Pets: **Yes**

5. Minnehaha County - W.H. Lyon Fairgrounds RV Park (Minnehaha County)

- **Location**: 100 N Lyon Blvd, Sioux Falls, SD 57107
- **GPS Coordinates**: 43.5560° N, 96.7603° W
- **Website**: W.H. Lyon Fairgrounds
- **Amenities**:
  ○ Full Hookups: **Yes**
  ○ Electric: **30/50 AMP**
  ○ Water: **Yes**
  ○ Pets: **Yes**

6. Brookings City Campground (City of Brookings)

- **Location: 2205 3rd St, Brookings, SD 57006**
- **GPS Coordinates: 44.3065° N, 96.7898° W**
- **Website: Brookings City Parks**
- **Amenities:**
  ○ **Full Hookups: Yes**
  ○ **Electric: 30/50 AMP**
  ○ **Water: Yes**
  ○ **Pets: Yes (leashed)**

7. Watertown City Park Campground (City of Watertown)

- **Location: 1910 W Kemp Ave, Watertown, SD 57201**
- **GPS Coordinates: 44.8994° N, 97.1301° W**
- **Website: Watertown Parks & Recreation**
- **Amenities:**
  - **Full Hookups: No**
  - **Electric: 30 AMP**
  - **Water: Yes**
  - **Pets: Yes**

8. Belle Fourche City Campground (City of Belle Fourche)

- **Location: 1111 National St, Belle Fourche, SD 57717**
- **GPS Coordinates: 44.6712° N, 103.8484° W**
- **Website: Belle Fourche Parks**
- **Amenities:**
  - **Full Hookups: Yes**
  - **Electric: 30/50 AMP**
  - **Water: Yes**
  - **Pets: Yes (with restrictions)**

9. Tea City Campground (City of Tea)

- **Location: 200 N Main Ave, Tea, SD 57064**
- **GPS Coordinates: 43.4461° N, 96.8358° W**
- **Website: City of Tea**
- **Amenities:**
  - **Full Hookups: No**
  - **Electric: 30 AMP**
  - **Water: Yes**
  - **Pets: Yes**

10. Vermillion City Campground (City of Vermillion)

- **Location: 202 E Main St, Vermillion, SD 57069**
- **GPS Coordinates: 42.7804° N, 96.9312° W**
- **Website: Vermillion Parks & Recreation**
- **Amenities:**
  - **Full Hookups: No**
  - **Electric: 30 AMP**
  - **Water: Yes**
  - **Pets: Yes**

TENNESSEE

County and Municipal RV Campgrounds in Tennessee

1. Cades Cove Campground (Blount County)

- **Location**: 10042 Campground Dr, Townsend, TN 37882
- **GPS Coordinates**: 35.6022° N, 83.7747° W
- **Website**: Blount County Parks
- **Amenities**:
  - Full Hookups: **No**
  - Electric: **30 AMP**
  - Water: **Yes**
  - Pets: **Yes** (with leash rules)

2. Sullivan County Campground (Sullivan County)

- **Location**: 3425 TN-126, Blountville, TN 37617
- **GPS Coordinates**: 36.5321° N, 82.3261° W
- **Website**: Sullivan County Parks
- **Amenities**:
  - Full Hookups: **No**
  - Electric: **30 AMP**
  - Water: **Yes**

○ Pets: **Yes**

3. Hamilton County – Chester Frost Park (Hamilton County)

- **Location**: 2277 Gold Point Cir N, Hixson, TN 37343
- **GPS Coordinates**: 35.1947° N, 85.1446° W
- **Website**: Chester Frost Park
- **Amenities**:
  ○ Full Hookups: **Yes**
  ○ Electric: **30/50 AMP**
  ○ Water: **Yes**
  ○ Pets: **Yes** (with leash rules)

4. Dandridge Municipal Park (Jefferson County)

- **Location**: 122 Public Dr, Dandridge, TN 37725
- **GPS Coordinates**: 36.0333° N, 83.4247° W
- **Website**: Dandridge Parks
- **Amenities**:
  ○ Full Hookups: **Yes**
  ○ Electric: **30/50 AMP**
  ○ Water: **Yes**
  ○ Pets: **Yes**

5. Paris Landing Campground (Henry County)

- **Location**: 16055 Hwy 79 N, Buchanan, TN 38222
- **GPS Coordinates**: 36.4361° N, 88.0831° W
- **Website**: Henry County Parks
- **Amenities**:
  ○ Full Hookups: **Yes**
  ○ Electric: **30/50 AMP**
  ○ Water: **Yes**
  ○ Pets: **Yes**

6. **Barfield Crescent Park Campground (Rutherford County)**

   - Location: 697 Veterans Pkwy, Murfreesboro, TN 37128
   - GPS Coordinates: 35.7901° N, 86.4415° W
   - Website: <u>Rutherford County Parks</u>
   - Amenities:
     - Full Hookups: No
     - Electric: 30 AMP
     - Water: Yes
     - Pets: Yes

7. **Billy Dunlop Park (Montgomery County)**

   - Location: 1930 E Boy Scout Rd, Clarksville, TN 37040
   - GPS Coordinates: 36.5666° N, 87.3327° W
   - Website: <u>Clarksville Parks & Rec</u>
   - Amenities:
     - Full Hookups: No
     - Electric: 30 AMP
     - Water: Yes
     - Pets: Yes

8. **Muse Park Campground (City of Jackson)**

   - Location: 80 Muse St, Jackson, TN 38301
   - GPS Coordinates: 35.6341° N, 88.8193° W
   - Website: <u>Jackson Parks</u>
   - Amenities:
     - Full Hookups: No
     - Electric: 30 AMP
     - Water: Yes
     - Pets: Yes

9. Fletcher Park Campground (Bradley County)

- Location: 2715 S Lee Hwy, Cleveland, TN 37311
- GPS Coordinates: 35.1232° N, 84.8834° W
- Website: Bradley County Parks
- Amenities:
  - Full Hookups: No
  - Electric: 30 AMP
  - Water: Yes
  - Pets: Yes

10. Maury County Park (Maury County)

- Location: 1018 Maury County Park Dr, Columbia, TN 38401
- GPS Coordinates: 35.6197° N, 87.0352° W
- Website: Maury County Parks
- Amenities:
  - Full Hookups: No
  - Electric: 30 AMP
  - Water: Yes
  - Pets: Yes

TEXAS

1. Galveston Island County Park (Galveston County)

- Location: 14901 FM3005, Galveston, TX 77554
- GPS Coordinates: 29.2108° N, 94.9370° W
- Website: Galveston Parks
- Amenities:
  - Full Hookups: Yes
  - Electric: 30/50 AMP
  - Water: Yes
  - Pets: Yes

2. Brazos County RV Park (Brazos County)

- **Location**: 3100 Highway 21 E, Bryan, TX 77803
- **GPS Coordinates**: 30.6808° N, 96.3669° W
- **Website**: <u>Brazos County Parks</u>
- **Amenities**:
  - Full Hookups: **Yes**
  - Electric: **30/50 AMP**
  - Water: **Yes**
  - Pets: **Yes**

3. Harris County - Deussen Park Campground (Harris County)

- **Location**: 12303 Sonnier St, Houston, TX 77044
- **GPS Coordinates**: 29.8954° N, 95.1404° W
- **Website**: <u>Harris County Parks</u>
- **Amenities**:
  - Full Hookups: **No**
  - Electric: **30 AMP**
  - Water: **Yes**
  - Pets: **Yes**

4. Denton City Water Works Park RV Area (Denton County)

- **Location**: 2400 Long Rd, Denton, TX 76207
- **GPS Coordinates**: 33.2302° N, 97.1301° W
- **Website**: <u>Denton Parks</u>
- **Amenities**:
  - Full Hookups: **Yes**
  - Electric: **30/50 AMP**
  - Water: **Yes**
  - Pets: **Yes**

5. San Angelo City - Spring Creek Marina & RV Park (Tom Green County)

- **Location**: 2680 Camper Rd, San Angelo, TX 76904
- **GPS Coordinates**: 31.3972° N, 100.4910° W
- **Website**: San Angelo Parks
- **Amenities**:
  - Full Hookups: **Yes**
  - Electric: **30/50 AMP**
  - Water: **Yes**
  - Pets: **Yes**

6. Lubbock County - Buffalo Springs Lake RV Park (Lubbock County)

- **Location**: 9999 High Meadow Rd, Lubbock, TX 79404
- **GPS Coordinates**: 33.5171° N, 101.7445° W
- **Website**: Buffalo Springs Lake
- **Amenities**:
  - Full Hookups: **Yes**
  - Electric: **30/50 AMP**
  - Water: **Yes**
  - Pets: **Yes**

7. Corpus Christi - Padre Balli Park (Nueces County)

- **Location**: 15820 Park Rd 22, Corpus Christi, TX 78418
- **GPS Coordinates**: 27.5804° N, 97.2245° W
- **Website**: Padre Balli Park
- **Amenities**:
  - Full Hookups: **Yes**
  - Electric: **30/50 AMP**
  - Water: **Yes**
  - Pets: **Yes**

8. Fort Bend County - Bates Allen Park

- Location: 9300 TX-36, Needville, TX 77461
- GPS Coordinates: 29.3843° N, 95.8410° W
- Website: Fort Bend County Parks
- Amenities:
  - Full Hookups: No
  - Electric: 30 AMP
  - Water: Yes
  - Pets: Yes

9. McKinney City - McKinney Campground

- Location: 111 N Tennessee St, McKinney, TX 75069
- GPS Coordinates: 33.1976° N, 96.6153° W
- Website: McKinney Parks
- Amenities:
  - Full Hookups: Yes
  - Electric: 30/50 AMP
  - Water: Yes
  - Pets: Yes

10. Arlington City - Richard Simpson Park

- Location: 6300 W Arkansas Ln, Arlington, TX 76016
- GPS Coordinates: 32.7053° N, 97.2185° W
- Website: Arlington Parks
- Amenities:
  - Full Hookups: No
  - Electric: 30 AMP
  - Water: Yes
  - Pets: Yes

11. Amarillo City - Thompson Park Campground

- Location: 2401 Dumas Dr, Amarillo, TX 79107
- GPS Coordinates: 35.2373° N, 101.8303° W
- Website: <u>Amarillo Parks</u>
- Amenities:
  - Full Hookups: Yes
  - Electric: 30/50 AMP
  - Water: Yes
  - Pets: Yes

12. Denton County - Lake Ray Roberts Marina

- Location: 1399 Marina Cir, Sanger, TX 76266
- GPS Coordinates: 33.3627° N, 97.0763° W
- Website: <u>Lake Ray Roberts</u>
- Amenities:
  - Full Hookups: Yes
  - Electric: 30/50 AMP
  - Water: Yes
  - Pets: Yes

13. Williamson County - Berry Springs Park & Preserve

- Location: 1801 Co Rd 152, Georgetown, TX 78626
- GPS Coordinates: 30.6861° N, 97.6350° W
- Website: <u>Williamson County Parks</u>
- Amenities:
  - Full Hookups: No
  - Electric: 30 AMP
  - Water: Yes
  - Pets: Yes

14. Hidalgo County - Delta Lake Park

- **Location: 2836 FM 88, Monte Alto, TX 78538**
- **GPS Coordinates: 26.4148° N, 97.9766° W**
- **Website: Hidalgo County Parks**
- **Amenities:**
  - **Full Hookups: Yes**
  - **Electric: 30/50 AMP**
  - **Water: Yes**
  - **Pets: Yes**

UTAH

County and Municipal RV Campgrounds in Utah

1. Spanish Fork River Park (Utah County)

- **Location**: 1750 N Main St, Spanish Fork, UT 84660
- **GPS Coordinates**: 40.1234° N, 111.6543° W
- **Website**: Spanish Fork Parks & Recreation
- **Amenities**:
  - Full Hookups: **Yes**
  - Electric: **30/50 AMP**
  - Water: **Yes**
  - Pets: **Yes** (with leash rules)

2. Weber County - Fort Buenaventura Park

- **Location**: 2450 A Ave, Ogden, UT 84401
- **GPS Coordinates**: 41.2224° N, 111.9746° W
- **Website**: Weber County Parks
- **Amenities**:
  - Full Hookups: **No**
  - Electric: **30 AMP**
  - Water: **Yes**

- Pets: **Yes**

3. Millard County Fairgrounds RV Park (Millard County)

- **Location**: 187 S Manzanita Ave, Delta, UT 84624
- **GPS Coordinates**: 39.3519° N, 112.5773° W
- **Website**: Millard County Parks
- **Amenities**:
  - Full Hookups: **Yes**
  - Electric: **30 AMP**
  - Water: **Yes**
  - Pets: **Yes**

4. Emery County - Huntington City Park

- **Location**: 100 N Main St, Huntington, UT 84528
- **GPS Coordinates**: 39.3306° N, 110.9647° W
- **Website**: Emery County Parks
- **Amenities**:
  - Full Hookups: **No**
  - Electric: **30 AMP**
  - Water: **Yes**
  - Pets: **Yes**

5. Carbon County Fairgrounds RV Park (Carbon County)

- **Location**: 450 S Fairgrounds Way, Price, UT 84501
- **GPS Coordinates**: 39.5951° N, 110.8107° W
- **Website**: Carbon County Parks
- **Amenities**:
  - Full Hookups: **Yes**
  - Electric: **30/50 AMP**
  - Water: **Yes**
  - Pets: **Yes**

6. Cache County Fairgrounds RV Park (Cache County)

- **Location**: 450 S 500 W, Logan, UT 84321
- **GPS Coordinates**: 41.7278° N, 111.8364° W
- **Website**: Cache County Parks
- **Amenities**:
  - Full Hookups: **No**
  - Electric: **30 AMP**
  - Water: **Yes**
  - Pets: **Yes**

7. Davis County - Legacy Events Center RV Park

- **Location**: 151 S 1100 W, Farmington, UT 84025
- **GPS Coordinates**: 40.9846° N, 111.8992° W
- **Website**: Davis County Parks
- **Amenities**:
  - Full Hookups: **Yes**
  - Electric: **30/50 AMP**
  - Water: **Yes**
  - Pets: **Yes**

8. Tooele County - Deseret Peak Complex RV Park

- **Location: 2930 W Hwy 112, Tooele, UT 84074**
- **GPS Coordinates: 40.5302° N, 112.3392° W**
- **Website: Tooele County Parks**
- **Amenities:**
  - Full Hookups: Yes
  - Electric: 30/50 AMP
  - Water: Yes
  - Pets: Yes

9. Wasatch County Event Center RV Park

- Location: 415 S Southfield Rd, Heber City, UT 84032
- GPS Coordinates: 40.5062° N, 111.4137° W
- Website: Wasatch County Parks
- Amenities:
  - Full Hookups: Yes
  - Electric: 30/50 AMP
  - Water: Yes
  - Pets: Yes

10. Box Elder County - Willard City RV Park

- Location: 80 N Main St, Willard, UT 84340
- GPS Coordinates: 41.4092° N, 112.0404° W
- Website: Box Elder County.
- Amenities:
  - Full Hookups: Yes
  - Electric: 30 AMP
  - Water: Yes
  - Pets: Yes

11. Juab County - Nephi City RV Park

- Location: 100 W 100 N, Nephi, UT 84648
- GPS Coordinates: 39.7119° N, 111.8363° W
- Website: Nephi City
- Amenities:
  - Full Hookups: No
  - Electric: 30 AMP
  - Water: Yes
  - Pets: Yes

12. Sevier County - Richfield City Park RV Area

- Location: 300 N Main St, Richfield, UT 84701
- GPS Coordinates: 38.7691° N, 112.0842° W
- Website: Sevier County Parks
- Amenities:
  - Full Hookups: No
  - Electric: 30 AMP
  - Water: Yes
  - Pets: Yes

UTAH

County and Municipal RV Campgrounds in Vermont

1. Lake Champagne Campground (Orange County)

- Location: 53 Lake Champagne Dr, Randolph Center, VT 05061
- GPS Coordinates: 43.9424° N, 72.6114° W
- Website: Lake Champagne Campground
- Amenities:
  - Full Hookups: Yes
  - Electric: 30/50 AMP
  - Water: Yes
  - Pets: Yes (with leash rules)

2. North Beach Campground (City of Burlington)

- Location: 60 Institute Rd, Burlington, VT 05408
- GPS Coordinates: 44.4915° N, 73.2342° W
- Website: North Beach Campground
- Amenities:
  - Full Hookups: No
  - Electric: 30 AMP

○ Water: Yes

○ Pets: Yes (pet-friendly policies)

3. Winhall Brook Campground (Bennington County)

- Location: 919 Winhall Station Rd, South Londonderry, VT 05155
- GPS Coordinates: 43.1726° N, 72.8053° W
- Website: Winhall Brook Campground
- Amenities:
  ○ Full Hookups: No
  ○ Electric: 30 AMP
  ○ Water: Yes
  ○ Pets: Yes

4. Grand Isle Campground (Grand Isle County)

- Location: 36 E Shore N, Grand Isle, VT 05458
- GPS Coordinates: 44.7191° N, 73.2975° W
- Website: Grand Isle Campground
- Amenities:
  ○ Full Hookups: No
  ○ Electric: 30/50 AMP
  ○ Water: Yes
  ○ Pets: Yes

VIRGINIA

County and Municipal RV Campgrounds in Virginia

1. Lake Fairfax Park (Fairfax County)

- Location: 1400 Lake Fairfax Dr, Reston, VA 20190
- GPS Coordinates: 38.9687° N, 77.3174° W
- Website: Lake Fairfax Park

- **Amenities**:
  - Full Hookups: **Yes**
  - Electric: **30/50 AMP**
  - Water: **Yes**
  - Pets: **Yes** (leash rules apply)

2. Chickahominy Riverfront Park (James City County)

- **Location**: 1350 John Tyler Hwy, Williamsburg, VA 23185
- **GPS Coordinates**: 37.2631° N, 76.8375° W
- **Website**: Chickahominy Riverfront Park
- **Amenities**:
  - Full Hookups: **Yes**
  - Electric: **30/50 AMP**
  - Water: **Yes**
  - Pets: **Yes**

3. Elizabeth Furnace Recreation Area (Shenandoah County)

- **Location**: 15618 Fort Valley Rd, Fort Valley, VA 22652
- **GPS Coordinates**: 38.9252° N, 78.3763° W
- **Website**: Elizabeth Furnace Recreation Area
- **Amenities**:
  - Full Hookups: **No**
  - Electric: **30 AMP**
  - Water: **Yes**
  - Pets: **Yes**

4. Newport News Park Campground (Newport News City)

- **Location**: 13560 Jefferson Ave, Newport News, VA 23603
- **GPS Coordinates**: 37.2007° N, 76.5488° W
- **Website**: Newport News Park
- **Amenities**:
  - Full Hookups: **No**

- Electric: **20/30 AMP**
- Water: **Yes**
- Pets: **Yes**

5. Pohick Bay Regional Park (Fairfax County)

- **Location: 6501 Pohick Bay Dr, Lorton, VA 22079**
- **GPS Coordinates: 38.6644° N, 77.1846° W**
- **Website: Pohick Bay Regional Park**
- **Amenities:**
  - **Full Hookups: Yes**
  - **Electric: 30/50 AMP**
  - **Water: Yes**
  - **Pets: Yes**

6. Bear Creek Lake Park (Cumberland County)

- **Location: 22 Bear Creek Lake Rd, Cumberland, VA 23040**
- **GPS Coordinates: 37.5317° N, 78.2733° W**
- **Website: Bear Creek Lake Park**
- **Amenities:**
  - **Full Hookups: No**
  - **Electric: 30 AMP**
  - **Water: Yes**
  - **Pets: Yes**

7. Prince William Forest RV Campground (Prince William County)

- **Location: 16058 Dumfries Rd, Dumfries, VA 22025**
- **GPS Coordinates: 38.5803° N, 77.3492° W**
- **Website: Prince William Forest RV Campground**
- **Amenities:**
  - **Full Hookups: Yes**
  - **Electric: 30/50 AMP**
  - **Water: Yes**

- Pets: Yes

8. Scott County Park & Golf Course (Scott County)

- **Location: 1497 Natural Tunnel Pkwy, Duffield, VA 24244**
- **GPS Coordinates: 36.7083° N, 82.7944° W**
- **Website: Scott County Park**
- **Amenities:**
  - **Full Hookups: No**
  - **Electric: 30 AMP**
  - **Water: Yes**
  - **Pets: Yes**

WASHINGTON

County and Municipal RV Campgrounds in Washington

1. Kayak Point Regional Park (Snohomish County)

- **Location**: 15610 Marine Dr, Stanwood, WA 98292
- **GPS Coordinates**: 48.1206° N, 122.3641° W
- **Website**: Snohomish County Parks
- **Amenities**:
  - Full Hookups: **No**
  - Electric: **30 AMP**
  - Water: **Yes**
  - Pets: **Yes**

2. Riverfront Park RV Park (Chelan County)

- **Location**: 1325 Walla Walla Ave, Wenatchee, WA 98801
- **GPS Coordinates**: 47.4187° N, 120.3133° W
- **Website**: City of Wenatchee
- **Amenities**:
  - Full Hookups: **Yes**

- Electric: **30/50 AMP**
- Water: **Yes**
- Pets: **Yes**

3. Camp Long (Seattle City Park)

- **Location**: 5200 35th Ave SW, Seattle, WA 98126
- **GPS Coordinates**: 47.5551° N, 122.3766° W
- **Website**: Seattle Parks
- **Amenities**:
  - Full Hookups: **No**
  - Electric: **20/30 AMP**
  - Water: **Yes**
  - Pets: **Yes** (on leash)

4. Yakima Sportsman State Park RV Campground (City of Yakima)

- **Location**: 904 University Pkwy, Yakima, WA 98907
- **GPS Coordinates**: 46.5867° N, 120.4684° W
- **Website**: City of Yakima
- **Amenities**:
  - Full Hookups: **Yes**
  - Electric: **30/50 AMP**
  - Water: **Yes**
  - Pets: **Yes**

5. Point Hudson Marina & RV Park (Jefferson County)

- **Location**: 103 Hudson St, Port Townsend, WA 98368
- **GPS Coordinates**: 48.1121° N, 122.7595° W
- **Website**: Port of Port Townsend
- **Amenities**:
  - Full Hookups: **Yes**
  - Electric: **30/50 AMP**
  - Water: **Yes**

- Pets: **Yes**

6. Squalicum Harbor Marina RV Park (Whatcom County)

- **Location**: 722 Coho Way, Bellingham, WA 98225
- **GPS Coordinates**: 48.7532° N, 122.5058° W
- **Website**: Port of Bellingham
- **Amenities**:
  - Full Hookups: **Yes**
  - Electric: **30/50 AMP**
  - Water: **Yes**
  - Pets: **Yes**

7. Howard Amon Park RV Campground (City of Richland)

- **Location: 500 Amon Park Dr, Richland, WA 99352**
- **GPS Coordinates: 46.2734° N, 119.2722° W**
- **Website: City of Richland Parks**
- **Amenities:**
  - **Full Hookups: No**
  - **Electric: 30 AMP**
  - **Water: Yes**
  - **Pets: Yes (leash required)**

8. Kenmore Waterfront Activities Center (City of Kenmore)

- **Location: 7353 NE 175th St, Kenmore, WA 98028**
- **GPS Coordinates: 47.7545° N, 122.2478° W**
- **Website: City of Kenmore**
- **Amenities:**
  - **Full Hookups: No**
  - **Electric: 30 AMP**
  - **Water: Yes**
  - **Pets: Yes**

9. Blue Lake Community Park (Grant County)

- Location: 34875 Park Lake Rd NE, Coulee City, WA 99115
- GPS Coordinates: 47.5889° N, 119.4073° W
- Website: Grant County Parks
- Amenities:
  - Full Hookups: Yes
  - Electric: 30/50 AMP
  - Water: Yes
  - Pets: Yes

10. Riverfront RV Park (City of Spokane)

- Location: 507 N Howard St, Spokane, WA 99201
- GPS Coordinates: 47.6600° N, 117.4250° W
- Website: City of Spokane Parks
- Amenities:
  - Full Hookups: No
  - Electric: 30 AMP
  - Water: Yes
  - Pets: Yes

11. Wenatchee Confluence State Park RV Area (City of Wenatchee)

- Location: 333 Olds Station Rd, Wenatchee, WA 98801
- GPS Coordinates: 47.4527° N, 120.3285° W
- Website: Wenatchee Parks
- Amenities:
  - Full Hookups: No
  - Electric: 30/50 AMP
  - Water: Yes
  - Pets: Yes

WEST VIRGINIA

County and Municipal RV Campgrounds in West Virginia

1. Jackson County Fairgrounds RV Park (Jackson County)

- **Location**: 121 Pinnell St, Cottageville, WV 25239
- **GPS Coordinates**: 38.8703° N, 81.8243° W
- **Website**: Jackson County Fairgrounds
- **Amenities**:
  - Full Hookups: **Yes**
  - Electric: **30/50 AMP**
  - Water: **Yes**
  - Pets: **Yes**

2. Mason County Fairgrounds Campground (Mason County)

- **Location**: 1277 Fairground Rd, Point Pleasant, WV 25550
- **GPS Coordinates**: 38.8555° N, 82.1341° W
- **Website**: Mason County Fairgrounds
- **Amenities**:
  - Full Hookups: **Yes**
  - Electric: **30/50 AMP**
  - Water: **Yes**
  - Pets: **Yes**

3. Barboursville Park Campground (Cabell County)

- **Location**: 809 County Rd 60/73, Barboursville, WV 25504
- **GPS Coordinates**: 38.4091° N, 82.2879° W
- **Website**: Barboursville Park
- **Amenities**:
  - Full Hookups: **No**
  - Electric: **30 AMP**
  - Water: **Yes**

o Pets: **Yes**

4. Holly Gray Park (Braxton County)

- **Location**: 105 Park Dr, Sutton, WV 26601
- **GPS Coordinates**: 38.6643° N, 80.6841° W
- **Website**: Braxton County Parks
- **Amenities**:
  o Full Hookups: **No**
  o Electric: **30 AMP**
  o Water: **Yes**
  o Pets: **Yes**

5. Mylan Park Campground (Monongalia County)

- **Location**: 500 Mylan Park Ln, Morgantown, WV 26501
- **GPS Coordinates**: 39.6455° N, 80.0026° W
- **Website**: Mylan Park
- **Amenities**:
  o Full Hookups: **Yes**
  o Electric: **30/50 AMP**
  o Water: **Yes**
  o Pets: **Yes**

6. Summit Bechtel Reserve (Fayette County)

- **Location**: 2550 Jack Furst Dr, Glen Jean, WV 25846
- **GPS Coordinates**: 37.9256° N, 81.1456° W
- **Website**: Summit Bechtel Reserve
- **Amenities**:
  o Full Hookups: **No**
  o Electric: **30/50 AMP**
  o Water: **Yes**
  o Pets: **Yes** (limited areas)

7. Kanawha County Parks - Coonskin Park

- **Location**: 2000 Coonskin Dr, Charleston, WV 25311
- **GPS Coordinates**: 38.3855° N, 81.5901° W
- **Website**: Kanawha County Parks
- **Amenities**:
  - Full Hookups: **No**
  - Electric: **30 AMP**
  - Water: **Yes**
  - Pets: **Yes** (leash required)

8. Marion County Fairgrounds

- **Location**: 2019 Fairmont Ave, Fairmont, WV 26554
- **GPS Coordinates**: 39.4832° N, 80.1418° W
- **Website**: Marion County Fair
- **Amenities**:
  - Full Hookups: **No**
  - Electric: **30 AMP**
  - Water: **Yes**
  - Pets: **Yes**

9. Brooke Hills Park (Brooke County)

- **Location**: 140 Gist Ln, Wellsburg, WV 26070
- **GPS Coordinates**: 40.2832° N, 80.6044° W
- **Website**: Brooke Hills Park
- **Amenities**:
  - Full Hookups: **No**
  - Electric: **30/50 AMP**
  - Water: **Yes**
  - Pets: **Yes**

10. Clay County Park

- **Location**: 504 Main St, Clay, WV 25043
- **GPS Coordinates**: 38.4640° N, 81.0832° W
- **Website**: Clay County Park
- **Amenities**:
  - Full Hookups: **No**
  - Electric: **30 AMP**
  - Water: **Yes**
  - Pets: **Yes**

11. Berkeley Springs - Warm Springs Municipal Campground

- **Location**: 334 Warm Springs Way, Berkeley Springs, WV 25411
- **GPS Coordinates**: 39.6265° N, 78.2295° W
- **Website**: Berkeley Springs
- **Amenities**:
  - Full Hookups: **No**
  - Electric: **30 AMP**
  - Water: **Yes**
  - Pets: **Yes**

WISCONSIN

County and Municipal RV Campgrounds in Wisconsin

1. Eau Claire County Expo Center Campground

- **Location**: 5530 Fairview Dr, Eau Claire, WI 54701
- **GPS Coordinates**: 44.7695° N, 91.4807° W
- **Website**: Eau Claire County Expo Center
- **Amenities**:
  - Full Hookups: **Yes**
  - Electric: **30/50 AMP**

- Water: **Yes**
- Pets: **Yes** (leash required)

2. Chippewa County - Lake Wissota County Park

- **Location**: 18127 County Hwy O, Chippewa Falls, WI 54729
- **GPS Coordinates**: 44.9364° N, 91.3024° W
- **Website**: Lake Wissota County Park
- **Amenities**:
  - Full Hookups: **No**
  - Electric: **30 AMP**
  - Water: **Yes**
  - Pets: **Yes**

3. Washington County - Glacier Hills County Park

- **Location**: 1664 Friess Lake Rd, Hubertus, WI 53033
- **GPS Coordinates**: 43.2832° N, 88.3431° W
- **Website**: Glacier Hills Park
- **Amenities**:
  - Full Hookups: **No**
  - Electric: **30 AMP**
  - Water: **Yes**
  - Pets: **Yes**

4. Waupaca County Fairgrounds RV Park

- **Location**: 602 South St, Waupaca, WI 54981
- **GPS Coordinates**: 44.3578° N, 89.0844° W
- **Website**: Waupaca County Fairgrounds
- **Amenities**:
  - Full Hookups: **Yes**
  - Electric: **30/50 AMP**
  - Water: **Yes**
  - Pets: **Yes**

5. Marathon County - Big Eau Pleine County Park

- **Location**: 135475 County Rd C, Stratford, WI 54484
- **GPS Coordinates**: 44.7814° N, 90.0289° W
- **Website**: Big Eau Pleine Park
- **Amenities**:
  - Full Hookups: **No**
  - Electric: **30 AMP**
  - Water: **Yes**
  - Pets: **Yes**

6. Brown County - Bay Shore Park Campground

- **Location: 5637 Sturgeon Bay Rd, New Franken, WI 54229**
- **GPS Coordinates: 44.6006° N, 87.8575° W**
- **Website: Brown County Parks**
- **Amenities:**
  - **Full Hookups: Yes**
  - **Electric: 30/50 AMP**
  - **Water: Yes**
  - **Pets: Yes (leash required)**

7. Racine County - Cliffside Park Campground

- **Location: 7320 Michna Rd, Racine, WI 53402**
- **GPS Coordinates: 42.7742° N, 87.7968° W**
- **Website: Racine County Parks**
- **Amenities:**
  - **Full Hookups: Yes**
  - **Electric: 30/50 AMP**
  - **Water: Yes**
  - **Pets: Yes**

8. Dane County - Lake Farm County Park

- Location: 4330 Libby Rd, Madison, WI 53711
- GPS Coordinates: 43.0275° N, 89.3303° W
- Website: Dane County Parks
- Amenities:
  - Full Hookups: No
  - Electric: 30 AMP
  - Water: Yes
  - Pets: Yes

9. La Crosse County - Veterans Memorial Campground

- Location: N4668 County Rd VP, West Salem, WI 54669
- GPS Coordinates: 43.8995° N, 91.1059° W
- Website: La Crosse County Parks
- Amenities:
  - Full Hookups: Yes
  - Electric: 30/50 AMP
  - Water: Yes
  - Pets: Yes

10. Vernon County - Sidie Hollow Park

- Location: E6051 County Rd XX, Viroqua, WI 54665
- GPS Coordinates: 43.5328° N, 90.8694° W
- Website: Vernon County Parks
- Amenities:
  - Full Hookups: No
  - Electric: 30 AMP
  - Water: Yes
  - Pets: Yes

11. Rock County - Sweet Allyn County Park

- **Location:** 3139 S Carver Rd, Janesville, WI 53546
- **GPS Coordinates:** 42.6667° N, 88.9871° W
- **Website:** Rock County Parks
- **Amenities:**
  - **Full Hookups: No**
  - **Electric: 30 AMP**
  - **Water: Yes**
  - **Pets: Yes**

WYOMING

County and Municipal RV Campgrounds in Wyoming

1. Riverton RV Park (Fremont County)

- **Location:** 1209 S Federal Blvd, Riverton, WY 82501
- **GPS Coordinates:** 43.0103° N, 108.3874° W
- **Website:** Riverton RV Park
- **Amenities:**
  - Full Hookups: **Yes**
  - Electric: **30/50 AMP**
  - Water: **Yes**
  - Pets: **Yes**

2. Buffalo City Park Campground (Johnson County)

- **Location:** 46 N Lobban Ave, Buffalo, WY 82834
- **GPS Coordinates:** 44.3486° N, 106.6985° W
- **Website:** City of Buffalo
- **Amenities:**
  - Full Hookups: **No**
  - Electric: **30 AMP**
  - Water: **Yes**

○ Pets: **Yes**

3. Cody City Park Campground (Park County)

- **Location**: 1402 Sheridan Ave, Cody, WY 82414
- **GPS Coordinates**: 44.5263° N, 109.0565° W
- **Website**: <u>City of Cody</u>.
- **Amenities**:
  ○ Full Hookups: **No**
  ○ Electric: **30/50 AMP**
  ○ Water: **Yes**
  ○ Pets: **Yes**

4. Douglas KOA Journey (Converse County)

- **Location**: 168 Cold Springs Rd, Douglas, WY 82633
- **GPS Coordinates**: 42.7623° N, 105.3604° W
- **Website**: Douglas KOA
- **Amenities**:
  ○ Full Hookups: **Yes**
  ○ Electric: **30/50 AMP**
  ○ Water: **Yes**
  ○ Pets: **Yes**

5. Pinedale RV Park (Sublette County)

- **Location**: 162 E Pine St, Pinedale, WY 82941
- **GPS Coordinates**: 42.8674° N, 109.8608° W
- **Website**: <u>Pinedale RV Park</u>
- **Amenities**:
  ○ Full Hookups: **Yes**
  ○ Electric: **30/50 AMP**
  ○ Water: **Yes**
  ○ Pets: **Yes**

6. Lander City Park (Fremont County)

- Location: 405 Fremont St, Lander, WY 82520
- GPS Coordinates: 42.8342° N, 108.7304° W
- Website: City of Lander
- Amenities:
  - Full Hookups: No
  - Electric: 30 AMP
  - Water: Yes
  - Pets: Yes

7. Gillette Fishing Lake Park (Campbell County)

- Location: 1447 W 4J Rd, Gillette, WY 82716
- GPS Coordinates: 44.2787° N, 105.5054° W
- Website: Campbell County Parks
- Amenities:
  - Full Hookups: No
  - Electric: 30 AMP
  - Water: Yes
  - Pets: Yes

8. Thermopolis Hot Springs RV Park (Hot Springs County)

- Location: 115 Big Springs Dr, Thermopolis, WY 82443
- GPS Coordinates: 43.6467° N, 108.2101° W
- Website: Thermopolis Tourism
- Amenities:
  - Full Hookups: Yes
  - Electric: 30/50 AMP
  - Water: Yes
  - Pets: Yes

9. Sheridan Lions Club Campground (Sheridan County)

- Location: 479 Brundage Ln, Sheridan, WY 82801
- GPS Coordinates: 44.7878° N, 106.9584° W
- Website: Visit Sheridan
- Amenities:
  - Full Hookups: No
  - Electric: 30 AMP
  - Water: Yes
  - Pets: Yes

10. Wheatland City Park (Platte County)

- Location: 800 9th St, Wheatland, WY 82201
- GPS Coordinates: 42.0553° N, 104.9556° W
- Website: Town of Wheatland
- Amenities:
  - Full Hookups: No
  - Electric: 30 AMP
  - Water: Yes
  - Pets: Yes

REFERENCES

15 Best State Park Campgrounds For RVers - RV LIFE https://rvlife.com/state-park-campgrounds/

A Complete Guide to RV Camping in State Parks of the ... https://wandrlymagazine.com/article/rv-camping-state-parks/

Packing Tips for Seasonal RV Trips https://explore.bookoutdoors.com/guides/packing-tips-for-seasonal-rv-trips/

The Beginner's Guide To Planning an RV Trip https://www.heremagazine.com/articles/rv-rental-road-trip-guide

Park Design Manual https://www.sdparks.org/content/dam/sdparks/en/pdf/Development/Park%20Design%20Manual.pdf

How to read a trail map https://www.bangordailynews.com/2024/08/11/outdoors/act-out/how-to-read-a-trail-map-joam40zk0w/

The Most Dog-Friendly State Park in Every State https://www.bringfido.com/blog/most-dog-friendly-state-park-in-every-state/

Camping Safety Tips for Setting up a Safe Campsite https://www.statefarm.com/simple-insights/auto-and-vehicles/simple-tips-for-camping-safety

RV Hookups: A Comprehensive Guide https://www.outdoorsy.com/blog/rv-hookups-a-comprehensive-guide

10 best state parks for camping and RVing https://10best.usatoday.com/awards/travel/best-state-park-for-rving-camping-2023/

8 Best Campgrounds for Kids in the West https://mwg.aaa.com/via/national-parks/best-campgrounds-kids

8 Best Pet-Friendly RV Destinations - This is Go RVing https://www.gorving.com/tips-inspiration/trip-planning/8-best-pet-friendly-rv-destinations

The 14 Best State Parks for Hiking in the U.S. https://www.outsideonline.com/adventure-travel/national-parks/best-state-parks-for-hiking/

Top Fishing Destinations in the US All 50 States https://fishanywhere.com/blog/top-fishing-destinations-in-the-us-all-50-states/

The Best Birding Hotspot in Every State https://www.birdsandblooms.com/travel/birding-hotspots/birding-every-state/

10 Best Scenic National Park Drives in the United States https://www.travelandleisure.com/trip-ideas/national-parks/best-national-park-drives

The 7 Principles - Leave No Trace Center for Outdoor Ethics https://lnt.org/why/7-principles/

Keep It Green: Tips for Eco-Friendly RV Camping https://www.teamford.ca/tools-resources/keep-it-green-tips-for-eco-friendly-rv-camping

RV Solar Panels: A Beginners Guide To Going Solar | Go RVing https://www.gorving.com/tips-inspiration/expert-advice/rv-solar-panels-beginners-guide-going-solar

246   REFERENCES

Role of Parks and Recreation in Conservation https://www.nrpa.org/our-work/Three-Pillars/role-of-parks-and-recreation-in-conservation/

Checklist for Your RV Camping First Aid Kit https://www.adventureincamping.com/blog/checklist-for-your-rv-camping-first-aid-kit/

The Ultimate Guide to an RV Emergency Travel Plan https://nationalvehicle.com/the-ultimate-guide-to-an-rv-emergency-plan/

Safety for Women Solo Camping https://solowomenrv.com/safety-for-women-solo-camping-2/

Animal Encounters - National Park Service https://www.nps.gov/mora/planyourvisit/upload/Animal-Encounters-Dec18.pdf

See a Sky Full of Stars at These Certified Dark-Sky Parks https://www.npca.org/articles/1806-see-a-sky-full-of-stars-at-these-certified-dark-sky-parks

Essential Photography Gear for Nature Photography https://visualwilderness.com/fieldwork/essential-photography-gear-for-nature-photography

RV Parks Giving Back: Community Support Activities That ... https://crrhospitality.com/blog/rv-parks-giving-back-community-support-activities-that-matter/

NYC's Top 10 Parks for Reflection and Meditation https://healthynyc.com/nycs-top-10-parks-for-reflection-and-meditation-2/

Geological Gems of State Parks https://www.parks.ca.gov/?page_id=29631

Escapees RV Club Member Benefits - Get The Most Out Of ... https://escapees.com/join/benefits/

What No One Tells You About Living In An RV Full-Time https://rvlife.com/living-in-an-rv-full-time-tips/

Take a Virtual Visit to a National Park https://www.nationalparks.org/connect/blog/take-virtual-visit-national-park

Made in United States
Orlando, FL
07 June 2025

61764630R00134